WHOLE WORLD
VEGETARIAN

WHOLE WORLD
VEGETARIAN
MARIE SIMMONS

PHOTOGRAPHY BY TERI LYNN FISHER AND JENNY PARK

A RUX MARTIN BOOK
HOUGHTON MIFFLIN HARCOURT
Boston New York 2016

Book design by Toni Tajima

Food styling by Jenny Park
Prop styling by Teri Lynn Fisher

Library of Congress Cataloging-in-Publication Data
Names: Simmons, Marie, author.
Title: Whole world vegetarian / Marie Simmons ;
    photography by Teri Lynn Fisher and Jenny Park.
Description: Boston : Houghton Mifflin Harcourt,
    2016. | "A Rux Martin book."
Identifiers: LCCN 2015044198 | ISBN 9780544018457
    (paperback)
Subjects: LCSH: Vegetarian cooking. | BISAC:
    COOKING / Vegetarian & Vegan. | COOKING
    / Regional & Ethnic / General. | COOKING /
    General. | LCGFT: Cookbooks.
Classification: LCC TX837 .S48683 2016 | DDC
    641.5/636—dc23
LC record available at http://lccn.loc.gov/2015044198

Printed in China
C&C 10 9 8 7 6 5 4 3 2 1

FOR STEPHANIE

ACKNOWLEDGMENTS

Once again the maxim "it takes a village" proves its point. Except in this case, it has taken much more than that. It has taken family, friends, neighbors, colleagues, and most of all, cooks from around the world. I thank all of you for your generosity of ideas and for your passion for cooking.

Before I get down to the nitty-gritty, I must thank my brilliant agent, Carole Bidnick, and her equal, my longtime and much-loved editor, Rux Martin.

A heartfelt thank-you to our talented photographers, artists, and stylists Teri Lynn Fisher and Jenny Park, and to the gifted designer Toni Tajima for creating such a beautiful cookbook. I love what you've done. On the same note, I am blown away by the clean, clear, sensible editing by Stephanie Fletcher. Somehow Stephanie managed to get into my head and give the recipes that "I'm your friend in the kitchen" voice that is so important in recipe writing. Thank you, Stephanie.

Getting down to the wire and fearing there was more to do than any mere mortal should have on her plate—plus the fact that my eyes were blurring—I owe a huge debt of gratitude to my good friends Brooke Jackson, Marcia Maffei, and Michele Postal for pitching in with recipe retesting and checking, and meticulous proofreading. Also, thank you to my granddaughter,

Seraphina; my daughter, Stephanie; my husband, John; my grandson, Joseph; and his dad, Shawn Wagner, for keeping me company in the kitchen and for pitching in with chopping and stirring from time to time.

Thank you to my Bay Area friends, Debbie Rugh and Kathleen O'Neill, for helping me source hard-to-find ingredients; Pam and Desmond Elder for sharing their son's amazing recipe for Jamaican Red Rice and Peas; and Kathleen de Wilbur, Paula Hamilton, Sue Ewing, and my sister, Patricia, for checking in from afar with encouragement and positive reinforcement when it was most needed. A special thanks to Peter Eberhart—newfound friend and soul mate—for his good appetite, good humor, and boundless enthusiasm and curiosity. To my neighbors Catherine Flynn-Purvis for her meticulous recipe testing and note taking; Barb May for her enthusiasm for recipe sharing and eating; and Alice Parman, John Zerzan, and Rick Postal, for being ready and willing to take a taste. And to my life-mate, John, for always being there with sensible solutions, moral support, and, of course, love.

Cold Potato, Beet, Carrot, and Pea Salad with Dill, page 153

CONTENTS

Mushroom Chilaquiles, page 246

INTRODUCTION

As I was taught in my Introduction to Anthropology, it is not just the Great Works of Mankind that make a culture. It is the daily things, like what people eat and how they serve it. —LAURIE COLWIN, *Home Cooking*

Decades ago, Atlantic Avenue, deep in the heart of Brooklyn, was a half-hour walk from my college campus, yet a world apart. I made the hike weekly to stock up on ingredients for my latest food passion: Middle Eastern food. Restaurants lined the avenue. Exotic music promised belly-dancing between courses. Persian carpets hung from walls, twinkling lights beckoned. Shish kebab, baba ghanouj, and hummus were on the menu.

Tucked between the restaurants lay Sahadi, a Middle Eastern bazaar of sorts. I ladled black, brown, and green olives from wooden barrels and hacked off blocks of milky white feta—their labels written in Arabic script—to take back to the dorm for lunch. Two doors away, at a Lebanese bakery, a conveyor belt creaked as it transported soft rounds of pita from the raging hot brick oven to nearby towers, ready to slip—still warm—into plastic bags. Long ovals of flatbread thick with crushed dried herbs—a heady mix of thyme, sumac, salt, and sesame seeds called za'atar—were stacked nearby.

This was food far beyond my mother's Italian kitchen, where we feasted on the best Italian-American food: baked stuffed artichokes, eggplant Parmigiano, and my grandmother's pillow-soft ricotta–stuffed ravioli with marinara sauce. I grew up in a family high on vegetables. As kids, we cut dandelion greens from fields, sat on the back porch eating fried squash blossoms like potato chips, chomped on carrots because they were good for our eyes, and swallowed our greens and cannellini beans flecked with garlic and swimming in olive oil because they would make us strong.

Early in the 1970s I became aware of something called the "vegetarian movement."

People ate vegetables. What was the big deal? I'd been doing that my entire life.

Over the years—as I traveled the world meeting chefs and cooks and discovering new recipes—more and more it seemed that the best and most interesting dishes were indeed vegetarian. Soon my new mantra became "whole world vegetarian." Fed by globalization, world vegetarian cuisine has been fueled by mass immigration and our insatiable desire for travel.

The movement has turned our supermarkets into international marketplaces, where you can buy tahini for your next batch of hummus and tins of smoked paprika for paella, then browse the imported Mexican cheese selection for an irresistible casserole of chilaquiles, the cheesy, gooey mélange of day-old tortillas and chile-laced tomato sauce. No longer requiring a hike to Atlantic Avenue in Brooklyn, bags of pita are tucked between rustic artisan loaves and sliced multigrain breads in the bakery section.

The American neighborhood is changing. At the Saturday market in Oregon, where I now live, local goat and sheep farmers offer feta so perfectly creamy with the right balance of sour and sweet that it makes my knees weak. Food carts bring us easy, inexpensive fare from all over the world. Mexican carts specialize in tortas, tacos, or tamales. Juanita, the proprietor of an El Salvadoran cart, makes luscious little masa harina patties that ooze melted cheese, beans, and sometimes, mashed potatoes. The Ethiopian proprietor of a nearby restaurant blows my mind with a perfectly seasoned fragrantly spiced vegetable stew.

These recipes—and more—set the stage for *Whole World Vegetarian*. I open my pantry of international ingredients and get to work roasting poblano chiles and tucking them into a big empanada filled with feta and green olives. Or I re-create an Indian version of "French toast" called egg toast from the streets of Delhi. When I'm in an Asian mood, I turn to the various forms of miso—fermented soybeans—to use as a glaze, in soup, or in salad dressing over crisp cooked green beans.

Whole World Vegetarian is for contemporary American cooks. It's a relaxed look at the dishes that have sustained and nurtured people from around the world no matter where their table happens to be. I have adapted, reinterpreted, and reinvented the recipes so you can make them seamlessly.

All you need is a slightly expanded pantry, a sharp knife, the soul of a cook—and an appetite.

Falafel Platter with Green Tahini Sauce, page 38

APPETIZERS AND SNACKS

Borani 16

Tahini and Beet Puree 19

Whipped Feta with Lemon and Oregano 20

Baba Ghanoush with Caramelized Onions 22

Roasted Red Pepper Spread with Hazelnuts and Smoked Paprika 25

Yogurt with Caramelized Onions 27

Eggplant and Tomato Dip with Turmeric 28

Sautéed Golden Haloumi 31

Spicy Fried Chickpeas 34

Mushroom and Roasted Poblano Quesadillas 36

Falafel Platter with Green Tahini Sauce 38

Mango and Mint Summer Rolls with Dipping Sauce 42

Arancini with Mushrooms, Peas, and Cheese 46

Borani

Borani esfanaaj is a popular spinach and yogurt dish from Iran. It has many variations, and can serve as a spread or dip depending on the thickness of the yogurt. The primary seasoning is peppermint. Both dried peppermint and fresh spearmint work, but I think the intensity of the dried mint adds the most flavor. When pomegranates are in season, garnish the dip with their glistening red seeds (these juicy red seeds inside the pomegranate are called arils). If they are not available, walnut pieces warmed in a little oil or butter also make a delicious topping. **MAKES 1½ CUPS; 4 SERVINGS**

- 1 pound large-leaf (from bunches, not bagged baby leaves) spinach, thick stems trimmed
- 2 tablespoons extra-virgin olive oil, plus more for drizzling
- ¼ cup broken walnuts (optional)
- ½ cup finely chopped red onion
- 1 teaspoon grated garlic
- ¾ cup plain whole-milk yogurt, preferably Greek style
- 2 tablespoons crumbled dried peppermint or 2 tablespoons finely chopped fresh mint
- ½ teaspoon coarse salt, or to taste
- ¼ cup pomegranate seeds (optional)
   Za'atar Flatbread (page 55) or warm pita, for serving

1 Place the spinach in a steaming basket set over boiling water and steam, covered, until limp, about 5 minutes. Lift the steamer from the saucepan and let the spinach stand until cool enough to handle. Use your hands to squeeze the moisture from the spinach or press it with the back of a spoon. (Save the spinach juice for soup or to drink for a quick pick-me-up.) Blot the spinach well in a kitchen towel to remove extra moisture.

2 Heat the oil in a medium skillet until hot enough to sizzle a piece of onion. If using the walnuts, add to the hot oil and sauté just until they begin to change color. Immediately remove with a slotted spoon to a side dish. Add all of the onion to the oil, reduce the heat to low, and sauté, stirring, until golden, 5 to 8 minutes. Stir in the garlic. Remove from the heat and reserve.

3 Add the spinach, yogurt, mint, and salt to the onion and stir until blended. Taste and add more salt, if needed. Spread the dip in a thin layer on a plate. Sprinkle the top with the walnuts or pomegranate seeds, if using, and drizzle with a thin stream of olive oil, if desired. Serve with the flatbreads or pita.

Tahini and Beet Puree

In this version of a favorite pureed beet dish, tahini, or Middle Eastern sesame paste, shares the stage with the cooked beets. The sweet earthy taste of the beets helps balance the slight bitterness of the tahini. Top this shocking pink puree with lots of fresh dill and mint or sprinkle with dukka, an addictive Egyptian blend of finely ground toasted almonds or hazelnuts, sesame seeds, cumin, and coriander. Spread the puree on toast or crackers, or serve as a dip with Baked Pita Chips (page 20), warmed soft pita, or vegetable crudités. If possible, make the puree a day to two ahead so the flavors will have time to develop. MAKES 2 CUPS; 6 SERVINGS

1 pound beets, scrubbed, green tops trimmed

⅓ cup tahini (see page 41)

1 tablespoon fresh lemon juice, or more to taste

1 garlic clove, grated or minced

1 teaspoon coarse salt, or more to taste

Finely chopped fresh mint or dill, for garnish (optional), or 2 tablespoons dukka (see page 27), for garnish (optional)

1 If the beets are large, peel them first with a vegetable peeler and then cut into large chunks. If they are small or medium, leave them whole or halve them. Place the beets in a steaming basket set over boiling water and steam, covered, until tender, 20 to 35 minutes depending on their size.

Lift the steamer from the saucepan and let the beets cool. When cool enough to handle, rub off the skins, if unpeeled, and trim the stem and blossom ends. Cut the beets into 1-inch chunks.

2 Combine the beets, tahini, lemon juice, garlic, and salt in a food processor and process until the puree is creamy and smooth, scraping down the sides every 30 seconds. It may take about 2 minutes or more for the mixture to become smooth. Taste and add more lemon juice or salt, if needed.

3 Scrape the puree into a bowl or storage container, cover, and refrigerate until ready to serve. Sprinkle with the mint or dill, if using, or dukka, before serving.

Whipped Feta with Lemon and Oregano

I use a favorite French sheep's-milk feta, readily available in my super-market, for this iconic Greek spread or dip. It is delicious with Baked Pita Chips, Crostini, or raw vegetables. Use your gutsiest extra-virgin olive oil (preferably Greek) to drizzle on top. Either fresh or dried oregano will work, although the fresh will be a bit mild compared to the intensity of the dried. **MAKES ABOUT 1¼ CUPS; 6 SERVINGS**

1 package (8 ounces) creamy feta cheese

¼ cup plain whole-milk Greek-style yogurt

2 tablespoons fruity extra-virgin olive oil, plus 1 tablespoon for garnish

1 teaspoon grated lemon zest

1 tablespoon fresh lemon juice

1 tablespoon finely chopped fresh oregano leaves or 1 teaspoon dried

Baked Pita Chips (see box), Crostini (page 23), or raw vegetables, for serving

1 Combine the feta, yogurt, 2 tablespoons of the oil, the lemon zest, and lemon juice in a food processor. Process until the mixture is creamy, scraping down the sides of the bowl at least once.

2 Use a rubber spatula to transfer the creamed feta mixture to a shallow bowl or serving dish, making ridges in the surface. Drizzle with the remaining 1 tablespoon oil so that it makes rivulets on the rough surface of the cheese. Sprinkle with the oregano, rubbing the dried leaves (if using) through your fingers to release the flavorful oils. Serve with the pita chips, crostini, or vegetables.

Baked Pita Chips

Preheat the oven to 350°F. Separate 6 rounds of pita (1 bag either whole wheat or white) along the folded edges to make flat circles. Brush the rough side of each lightly with olive oil and sprinkle lightly with salt, za'atar (see page 32), or smoked paprika, preferably pimentón de la Vera (see page 26), or leave plain. Stack 2 or 3 of the circles at a time and cut into 6 pie-shaped wedges. Spread the wedges on baking sheets and bake until golden, 12 to 15 minutes. Stored in a resealable plastic bag, the pita chips will keep for up to 2 weeks.

Baba Ghanoush
with Caramelized Onions

I'm a big fan of baba ghanoush, grilled or roasted eggplant pureed with tahini. This one, made with sautéed caramelized onions, has a slightly sweeter flavor than many other versions. I prefer to roast the eggplants on the grill, but "roasting" under the broiler works, too, and is often more practical. MAKES 2½ TO 3 CUPS; 6 TO 8 SERVINGS

2 medium eggplants (about 15 ounces each), pierced all over with the tines of a fork

2 tablespoons extra-virgin olive oil, plus 1 tablespoon more for drizzling

1 cup finely chopped onion

1 garlic clove, grated

½ teaspoon ground cumin

¼ cup tahini (see page 41)

3 to 4 tablespoons fresh lemon juice, to taste

1 teaspoon hot ajvar (Turkish vegetable and pepper paste; see page 23) or harissa (see page 72), or more to taste

½ teaspoon coarse salt, or more to taste

1 tablespoon finely chopped fresh mint, parsley, and/or dill

Crostini (page 23), Baked Pita Chips (page 20), and/or raw vegetables, for serving

1 Place the eggplants on a piece of foil large enough to wrap them after they have been charred. Slide the foil onto a baking sheet. Preheat the broiler and position the baking sheet on a shelf so the eggplants are about 3 inches from the heat source. Broil the eggplants, turning as needed, until the skins are wrinkled and charred and the eggplants are very soft, about 25 minutes. Remove from the broiler, wrap in the foil, and let cool to room temperature.

2 Heat the 2 tablespoons oil in a medium skillet until hot enough to sizzle a piece of onion. Add the onion and cook, stirring, over medium-low heat until the onion is softened and lightly browned, about 20 minutes. Stir in the garlic and cumin and cook, stirring, for about 1 minute. Remove from the heat.

3 Peel the skin from the cooled eggplants and discard. Halve the eggplants and if there are lobes of dark seeds in the center, lift them out with a spoon and discard. Small, light-colored seeds can be left in. Coarsely chop the eggplant.

4 In a food processor, combine the eggplant, onion, tahini, lemon juice, pepper paste, and salt. Pulse just to combine. Do not make it too smooth; the texture should be rough. Taste and add more salt and pepper paste, if desired.

5 Spread the mixture on a large plate or in a shallow bowl. Drizzle the top with the remaining 1 tablespoon oil and sprinkle with the herbs. Serve with the crostini, pita chips, or vegetables for dipping.

Hot Ajvar, or Turkish Vegetable and Pepper Paste

Available wherever Middle Eastern products are sold and in some supermarkets with a good selection of ethnic ingredients, hot ajvar is a mixture of vegetables and peppers, some hot, cooked down to a paste. The intensity of heat varies among brands, so it is a good idea to taste before using. It comes in a 12-ounce jar. Once you open it, add a $1/4$-inch layer of olive oil over the top to help keep the paste fresh. If unavailable, substitute harissa (see page 72), available wherever Middle Eastern groceries are sold, but proceed cautiously, tasting after each 1 teaspoon addition, as it can be very hot.

Crostini

Whenever I have a partially used loaf of day-old Italian bread or French baguette, I cut it into $1/4$- to $1/2$-inch-thick slices, brush the slices lightly with olive oil, and bake them in a preheated 350°F oven until golden, 15 to 20 minutes. (Do not use sourdough bread; the toasts will be too hard and brittle.) Stored in a resealable plastic bag, these crostini will keep for a week or two and come in handy as a snack with spreads and dips.

Roasted Red Pepper Spread with Hazelnuts and Smoked Paprika

Inspired by a favorite recipe for muhammarra, the now ubiquitous puree made with roasted red peppers, walnuts, and pomegranate molasses, this spread pays homage to Turkey's hazelnut industry (Turkey is the largest producer worldwide) and Spain's smoked paprika, or pimentón de la Vera, a type of sweet paprika with a complex smoked wood aroma and taste. You can toast and peel a large batch of hazelnuts ahead of time and store them in the freezer (hazelnuts are perishable). **MAKES 1½ CUPS; 6 SERVINGS**

1 cup hazelnuts, plus a few extra for garnish

1 jar (12 ounces) roasted and peeled red peppers, rinsed, drained, and coarsely chopped, or 2 red bell peppers

1 thin slice fresh whole-grain bread, crumbled (½ cup)

2 tablespoons pomegranate molasses (see page 26)

1 teaspoon coarse salt

1 teaspoon smoked paprika, preferably pimentón de la Vera (see page 26)

1 teaspoon hot ajvar (Turkish vegetable and pepper paste; see page 23), or harissa (see page 72), or more to taste

½ teaspoon ground cumin

¼ teaspoon cayenne pepper, or to taste

½ cup extra-virgin olive oil

Baked Pita Chips (page 20) and raw vegetables, such as celery, green bell peppers, peeled carrots, or fennel, for serving

1 Preheat the oven to 350°F. Spread the hazelnuts in a shallow baking dish or pan and roast until the skins are cracked and a shade darker, 18 to 20 minutes. Pour the hot hazelnuts into a large kitchen towel, gather it together, and let stand until the hazelnuts are cool, about 30 minutes. Rub the towel vigorously so the friction of the nuts and the towel loosens and removes the skins. Pick the nuts out and use at once, or freeze for future use.

2 If using fresh bell peppers, preheat the broiler. Place the peppers on a large sheet of aluminum foil and place on a baking sheet. Position the pan so the peppers are about 2 inches from the heat source. Broil, turning as needed, until the peppers are evenly charred, about 5 minutes per side. Remove from the broiler and wrap the peppers in the foil. When the peppers are cool enough to handle, pull off the charred skins. Split the peppers and remove the stems, seeds, and ribs. Reserve any pepper juices in the foil. Pat the peppers dry and coarsely chop.

3 Finely chop 1 cup of the hazelnuts in a food processor. Add the roasted peppers, reserved pepper juices on the foil, if any, bread, pomegranate molasses, salt, paprika, pepper paste, cumin, and cayenne. Add the oil in a thin steady stream while pulsing the food processor. Pulse until the mixture is pureed.

4 Spread the puree on a serving plate. Coarsely chop the reserved hazelnuts and sprinkle on top. Serve with the pita chips and vegetables for dipping.

Pomegranate Molasses

This sweet and tart condiment, available in bottles wherever Middle Eastern groceries are sold, is a thick, pourable reduction of pure pomegranate juice. It is also sometimes called syrup or paste. The bottle does not have to be refrigerated, even after opening.

Pimentón de la Vera

This smoky sweet paprika with an almost meaty taste comes from an area in Spain called La Vera, where the chiles are roasted and dried over a wood fire before being ground. It comes in three forms: *dulce,* or sweet; *agridulce,* or spicy-sweet; and *piccante,* or hot. My favorite is the *dulce,* and I use it in many dishes. It is available in most supermarkets and in specialty food shops. If the imported Spanish pimentón de la Vera is not available, any smoked paprika, now widely available, is a good substitute.

Yogurt with Caramelized Onions

In this creamy mixture of yogurt and cooked onions, the onions become soft and caramelized, turning the tangy yogurt from sour to sweet. The mixture is good on warm pita by itself, or sprinkled with chopped fresh mint, ground sumac or za'atar, dukka, or, in season, pomegranate seeds.

MAKES 1½ CUPS; 6 SERVINGS

2 tablespoons extra-virgin olive oil

1 cup chopped onion

½ teaspoon coarse salt, or more to taste

1½ cups plain whole-milk yogurt, preferably Greek style

Chopped fresh mint leaves (optional)

Pomegranate seeds (optional)

Za'atar (see page 32), dukka (see box), or sumac (see box; optional)

Warm pita, for serving

1 In a medium skillet, heat the oil until hot enough to sizzle a piece of onion. Add the onion and cook, stirring, over medium to medium-low heat until the onion is very soft and a light golden in color, about 10 minutes. Remove from the heat and let stand until cooled. Stir in the salt.

2 In a bowl, stir together the cooked onions and the yogurt until blended. Serve at room temperature or chilled. Garnish with mint; a few pomegranate seeds; or a sprinkling of za'atar, dukka, or sumac, and serve with warm pita.

Sumac

Not the poisonous kind, this variety of sumac is a citrusy-tasting seasoning made from berries that are sun-dried on their branches and then ground into a coarse powder. Usually dark red in color, it is delicious sprinkled on plain yogurt. It is available wherever Middle Eastern groceries are sold and online (see Sources, page 308). For color you can use fresh pomegranate seeds, but they won't add the distinctive taste of dried sumac.

Dukka

Dukka—an Egyptian condiment—is a blend of ground almonds or hazelnuts, sesame seeds, cumin, and coriander that have each been lightly toasted in a small skillet and then stirred together. It is delicious sprinkled on cooked vegetables, as a dip for olive oil–soaked flatbread, or as a topping for plain yogurt. Dukka is sold in small bags in the spice section of ethnic markets and well-stocked supermarkets.

Eggplant and Tomato Dip with Turmeric

This is hearty enough to make a meal when served with halved hard-cooked eggs, crumbled feta cheese, and an assortment of olives. Ground crushed Aleppo pepper adds a rich, meaty taste—but not much heat—to the overall dish. MAKES ABOUT 3 CUPS; 6 TO 8 SERVINGS

1½ pounds (2 medium) eggplant, pierced all over with the tines of a sharp fork

2 or 3 large ripe tomatoes or 1½ cups whole canned tomatoes with their juices

¼ cup extra-virgin olive oil

4 garlic cloves, chopped

2 tablespoons canned tomato paste

1 teaspoon turmeric

1 teaspoon crushed Aleppo pepper (optional; see page 40)

1 teaspoon coarse salt, plus more to taste

Pinch of cayenne pepper or other ground red chile pepper, or more to taste

2 or 3 sprigs fresh dill

2 or 3 sprigs fresh mint

2 or 3 sprigs fresh flat-leaf (Italian) parsley

½ cup assorted black and/or green olives, preferably pitted, for serving (optional)

Hard-cooked eggs, for serving (optional)

Warm pita or flatbread, for serving (optional)

1 Preheat the oven to 400°F, or preheat a grill. Place the eggplants on a piece of foil large enough to wrap them after they are softened. Roast the eggplants on a baking sheet in the oven, or on the grill, turning about every 20 minutes, until the skin is wrinkled (and in the case of the grill, charred) and the eggplant is softened throughout, about 45 minutes in the oven or 30 minutes on the grill. Remove from the oven, wrap in foil, and let cool. When cool enough to handle, peel off the skin and cut up the eggplant, removing any thick sacks of dark seeds. Coarsely chop the cooked eggplant and set aside.

2 Meanwhile, if using fresh tomatoes, cut an X in the blossom end of each and plunge the tomatoes into a saucepan of boiling water. When the tomato skins begin to peel back, lift the tomatoes out of the water with a slotted spoon and let them cool slightly on a plate. Peel off the skins and squeeze the tomatoes with your hands, or finely chop in a food processor. You should have about 1½ cups tomato puree. If ripe tomatoes aren't available, puree the canned tomatoes in a food processor or blender.

3 Heat the oil and garlic in a large skillet over medium heat until the garlic starts to sizzle. Do not brown the garlic. Immediately

add the eggplant, tomatoes, tomato paste, turmeric, Aleppo pepper (if using), salt, and cayenne. Cook, stirring, over medium to medium-low heat until the liquid is cooked down and the mixture is very thick, about 15 minutes.

4 Meanwhile, finely chop the dill, mint, and parsley together to measure a total of about ¼ cup. Add half of the herbs to the tomato and eggplant spread. Taste and add more salt and cayenne, if needed. Remove from the heat and let cool to room temperature.

5 Spread the tomato and eggplant mixture on a platter and sprinkle with the reserved half of the chopped herbs. Garnish the platter with the olives and hard-cooked eggs, if serving as a main course, and serve with the pita or flatbread. Serve the eggplant mixture at room temperature or chilled.

Sautéed Golden Haloumi

This cheese is described in my well-worn copy of *Murray's Cheese Book* as "a rubbery little block, off white and tightly wrapped in Cryovac, not usually what we'd associate with fine cheese. But in the proper application, haloumi is irreplaceable." The following recipe is, I'd argue, the "proper application." The version most readily found at many cheese counters is usually enjoyed pan-fried or grilled. Hot off the grill or pan, the outside is firm and crunchy and the inside irresistibly soft and runny. As it cools, the inside turns "squeaky." I like it with a simple topping of an intensely fruity olive oil and some lemon juice, zipped up with a teaspoon or two of za'atar, the Middle Eastern spice blend of sumac, thyme, and sesame seeds. A more traditional embellishment is a drizzle of olive oil and a sprinkling of toasted pignoli. In the following versions, I describe how to cook the cheese plain, coated with flour, or coated with panko crumbs. Each is delicious. The haloumi is best when soaked in cold water for at least 1 hour or overnight before using. MAKES 4 SERVINGS

1 package (about 12 ounces) haloumi, split lengthwise into 2 pieces

¼ cup all-purpose flour

1 large egg, beaten

¼ cup panko bread crumbs

Extra-virgin olive oil, as needed, for frying

Extra-Virgin Olive Oil, Lemon, and Za'atar Topping (optional; recipe follows) or Extra-Virgin Olive Oil and Toasted Pignoli Topping (optional; recipe follows)

1 Unwrap the haloumi, rinse well under cold water, and place in a bowl. Add cold water to cover and soak for at least 1 hour or as long as overnight. The soaking will help remove some of the saltiness and will add extra moisture. Drain and pat dry with a kitchen towel.

2 You can fry the cheese plain, or you can coat it first in flour or in bread crumbs. If using only flour, sprinkle it on a small plate and turn the cheese in the flour until evenly coated. Alternatively, to coat with panko bread crumbs, coat the cheese first with the flour, then dip in the beaten egg, allowing the excess to drip off, and finally roll in the panko, pressing the panko into the cheese with your fingertips. Set aside until ready to fry.

3 Heat about ¼ inch of oil in a heavy skillet large enough to hold the 2 pieces

of cheese. When the oil is hot enough to sizzle a bread crumb, add the cheese (plain, flour-coated, or panko-coated) and fry until golden brown on one side, 1 to 2 minutes. Carefully turn with a wide spatula and a fork (to avoid splattering) and cook until the other side is browned, 1 to 2 minutes more.

4 Transfer to a serving platter and eat plain or with the topping of your choice while the cheese is still hot.

Extra-Virgin Olive Oil, Lemon, and Za'atar Topping

In a small bowl, whisk 2 tablespoons extra-virgin olive oil, ½ tablespoon fresh lemon juice, and 2 teaspoons za'atar (see box) until blended. Spoon over the hot haloumi.

Extra-Virgin Olive Oil and Toasted Pignoli Topping

To toast the pignoli, preheat the oven to 350°F. Spread the pignoli in a shallow pan and bake until evenly browned, 10 to 15 minutes. Drizzle 1 to 2 tablespoons extra-virgin olive oil over the hot haloumi and sprinkle with 2 tablespoons toasted pignoli.

Za'atar

Za'atar is a mixture of spices (dried thyme and sometimes oregano or marjoram, dried sumac, and toasted sesame seeds). I first tasted it many years ago in my favorite bakery on Atlantic Avenue in Brooklyn, New York. There, it was liberally sprinkled on a long, thin, soft spongy bread that was folded into thirds and slipped, while still warm, into a plastic bag. Za'atar is available in bags or bottles wherever Middle Eastern groceries are sold and online (see Sources, page 308). **To make your own version:** Combine 2 teaspoons dried thyme, 2 teaspoons dried oregano, 2 teaspoons toasted sesame seeds, 2 teaspoons dried sumac, and ¹/₂ teaspoon salt.

Spicy Fried Chickpeas

For this appetizer, a popular street food in Sri Lanka, the chickpeas should be very dry before they are fried. I usually spread them on a towel and let them air-dry for several hours or overnight. Most recipes have you add the chickpeas to the oil last, but I prefer to fry them first so the outside turns crunchy. Fresh curry leaves can be hard to find. They have a distinctive taste, and there really is no substitute. When I can't find them in my Asian or Indian market, I simply leave them out. **MAKES 4 TO 6 SERVINGS**

2 cups cooked dried or canned chickpeas, drained

¼ cup vegetable oil

1 teaspoon black or brown mustard seeds (see page 100)

¼ cup finely chopped shallot or onion

1 garlic clove, finely chopped

1 teaspoon coarse salt

½ teaspoon crushed red pepper flakes, or to taste

½ teaspoon ground turmeric

1 whole curry leaf (optional; see box)

1 Lay out a kitchen towel on a baking sheet and spread the chickpeas on the towel. Let stand, at room temperature, to air-dry the chickpeas, several hours or overnight.

2 Heat the oil in a medium skillet over medium heat. Add the mustard seeds and cook, stirring, until the seeds begin to pop.

Immediately add the chickpeas. Turn the heat to high and stir-fry the chickpeas until they are golden and crisp, about 10 minutes.

3 Add the shallot, garlic, salt, red pepper flakes, turmeric, and curry leaf (if using) and cook, stirring, over medium to medium-low heat until the shallot is golden, about 5 minutes. Serve the chickpeas warm or at room temperature.

Curry Leaf

From a plant native to Southern Asia, curry leaf is highly fragrant, with a pungent currylike aroma. It looks like a lemon leaf and is available fresh in Indian markets. In an airtight container, curry leaves will keep, refrigerated, for about 2 weeks. There is really no substitute. You could simply omit it from the recipe or, if you prefer, you can use another herb, perhaps fresh basil.

Mushroom and Roasted Poblano Quesadillas

A mélange of different mushrooms are marketed as "exotic" in some super-markets. I sometimes indulge in small boxes consisting of shiitake, cremini, and oyster mushrooms, but I am happiest when I can find all of these mushrooms plus others sold in bulk. Then I can mix and match, adding a few hedgehogs, a nice meaty matsutake, or, in season, a few local chanterelles or other varieties. Then I nestle the stir-fry in a bed of hot oozy cheese, made piquant with roasted poblano chiles. **MAKES 4 SERVINGS**

2 large poblano chiles

12 ounces mixed mushrooms, such as shiitake, hedgehog, oyster, matsutake, cremini, or other exotics

3 tablespoons extra-virgin olive oil, plus more as needed

½ cup thinly sliced (lengthwise) onion

¾ teaspoon chile powder

Coarse salt

1 garlic clove, grated

4 (8-inch) flour tortillas

1 cup shredded Oaxaca (see page 249), mozzarella, Manchego (see page 65), or Monterey Jack cheese

1 Preheat the broiler. Line a baking sheet with foil and place the poblanos on the foil. Set the baking sheet on the shelf about 2 to 3 inches from the heat source and broil, turning the peppers as they blister and char, for 3 to 5 minutes per side. Remove from the broiler and wrap in the foil. When cool enough to handle, unwrap the chiles and rub off the charred skins. Split the chiles in half and remove and discard the stems and seeds. You will have 4 halves of roasted peeled chiles. Blot the halves with paper towels and set aside.

2 Remove and discard the tough stems from the shiitakes, if using. Coarsely chop all of the mushrooms into ¼- to ½-inch pieces, caps and tender stems included. You should have about 4 cups raw mushrooms.

3 Heat 1 tablespoon of the oil in a 10-inch skillet until hot enough to sizzle a piece of onion. Add all the onion and cook, stirring, over medium to medium-low heat until golden, about 5 minutes. Stir in the chile powder and a sprinkling of salt. Transfer to a dish and reserve. Wipe out the skillet.

4 Add the remaining 2 tablespoons oil to the skillet and heat until hot enough to sizzle a piece of mushroom. Add all of the mushrooms and cook, stirring, until the mushrooms are tender and any moisture has cooked off, 8 to 10 minutes. Stir in the garlic and a sprinkling of salt. Add the reserved onion mixture and stir until well blended. Remove from the heat.

5 Lightly brush the undersides of 4 tortillas with a thin film of oil. Place the oiled side down on a work surface. Lay a poblano chile half on the lower half of each tortilla. Top with about 2 tablespoons of cheese. Top each half with about one quarter of the mushroom mixture, distributing evenly. Then top with the remaining cheese, about 2 tablespoons for each tortilla. Fold the top half of the tortilla over the filling and lightly press it down.

6 Heat the skillet over medium heat until hot enough to sizzle a drop of water. Place 2 of the quesadillas—with the folded edges toward the center—in the skillet. Cook until the bottoms are golden, about 5 minutes. Use a wide pancake turner to flip the quesadillas and cook until the other side is browned, about 5 minutes. Remove from the heat and let stand in the hot pan for 5 minutes. Transfer to a platter and cut each quesadilla into 3 wedges. Repeat with the remaining 2 quesadillas.

Falafel Platter with Green Tahini Sauce

I was introduced to falafel decades ago on Atlantic Avenue, in Brooklyn, New York, which at the time was a stretch of Middle Eastern shops and restaurants. At the neighborhood falafel shop, the balls, scooped from big vats of batter, were deep-fried to order and then plopped into warm pita, topped with chopped lettuce, tomatoes, and herbs, and liberally squirted with tahini sauce and, if desired, another squirt of hot sauce. That falafel is my benchmark for all others, and after years of experimenting, this recipe is about as close as I can get. But here, I suggest serving the falafel on a "platter" of lettuce instead of as a sandwich. The falafel are best eaten freshly fried, so have all the platter ingredients, including the Green Tahini Sauce, at the ready before frying the falafel. MAKES 4 SERVINGS

1 cup dried chickpeas (see page 40)

½ cup chopped onion

½ cup chopped packed fresh flat-leaf (Italian) parsley, including tender stems

¼ cup chopped packed fresh cilantro, including tender stems, plus sprigs for garnish (optional)

¼ cup thinly sliced scallion (green and white parts)

1 tablespoon chopped garlic

1½ teaspoons coarse salt

1 teaspoon crushed Aleppo pepper (see page 40), or to taste, or a pinch of crushed red pepper flakes

1 teaspoon ground cumin

½ teaspoon ground coriander

½ teaspoon baking powder

¼ teaspoon cayenne pepper, or to taste

2 tablespoons tahini (see page 41), or as needed

All-purpose flour, as needed to coat the balls

Vegetable oil, as needed for frying

2 cups thinly sliced romaine or other lettuce

2 ripe tomatoes, cored and cut into ½-inch chunks

1 cucumber, peeled and thinly sliced

Green Tahini Sauce (page 41)

4 pita, warmed (optional)

1 Place the chickpeas in a bowl and add water to cover by 2 inches. Let stand, covered, for at least 6 to 8 hours or overnight. Drain well. Spread the chickpeas on a kitchen towel and pat dry.

2 Place the chickpeas, onion, parsley, cilantro, scallion, garlic, salt, Aleppo pepper, cumin, coriander, baking powder, and

cayenne in a food processor. Process the chickpea mixture, scraping down the sides of the bowl as needed, until the mixture is finely ground and comes together. Add the tahini and process until the mixture is pasty enough to hold together in a small ball about the size of a walnut.

3 Spread about ½ cup of flour on a plate or large piece of wax paper. With dampened hands, gently shape the chickpea mixture into about 16 balls. Handle the mixture gently and do not squeeze the balls. Roll the balls, one at a time, in the flour. Hold the ball gently in your hand with your fingers spread and shake the ball so excess flour will fall away. Line up the balls on a tray as they are formed.

4 Heat about 1 inch of oil in a 10- or 12-inch heavy skillet until hot enough to sizzle and brown a small piece of falafel. Add one ball, as a test, and fry for 4 minutes. Gently turn with a slotted spoon and fry for about 4 minutes more, until all sides are browned. If the timing works, the oil is ready. Fry 4 to 6 balls at a time, gently turning with a spoon. Have ready a tray or a plate lined with a double layer of paper towels to drain the balls as they are fried.

5 Spread the lettuce on a platter, top with the tomatoes and cucumber, and then drizzle with about ¼ cup of the Green Tahini Sauce. Arrange the hot falafel on top. Garnish with sprigs of cilantro, if using. Serve with warm pita, if desired, adding more sauce for serving, as desired.

Chickpeas for Falafel

It's important to use dried chickpeas, not canned. Soak the dried chickpeas for 6 to 8 hours or overnight before using, but do not cook them. The reconstituted dried chickpeas will have just enough moisture in them to produce a tender, fluffy falafel that is crisp on the outside. Canned or cooked dried chickpeas are too moist to produce the right texture.

Aleppo Pepper

This mild pepper, with a rich, meaty taste but little heat, is named after a city in Syria. Dried and coarsely ground or crushed into flakes, it is used to flavor breads—sprinkle it on flatbread (page 55) or Baked Pita Chips (page 20)—and in savory dishes. It is available in jars or bags wherever Middle Eastern groceries are sold or online (see Sources, page 308). In a pinch substitute smoked paprika, to taste.

Green Tahini Sauce

This rich, smooth "sauce" has the consistency of fluffy mayonnaise, but it's the taste of fresh cilantro that wins the day. It's a sauce for dipping, made with bunches of cilantro and parsley pureed into the tahini with lemon juice and salt. Spoon blobs over the falafel or onto the side of your plate and dip falafel into the sauce between bites. If you choose to go the stuffed pita route, spread the Green Tahini Sauce on the pita before adding the falafel to the sandwich. MAKES ABOUT 2½ CUPS

1 cup packed coarsely chopped fresh flat-leaf (Italian) parsley, including tender stems

1 cup packed coarsely chopped fresh cilantro, including tender stems

1 garlic clove, chopped

1 teaspoon coarse salt, or more to taste

1 cup tahini (see box)

3 tablespoons fresh lemon juice, or more to taste

1 cup cold water, plus more as needed

½ teaspoon Tabasco or other hot pepper sauce, or to taste

1 In a food processor, finely chop the parsley, cilantro, garlic, and salt. Add the tahini and lemon juice and process until the herbs are very fine and turn the sauce a pale green. The tahini will seize up and turn pastelike. With the motor running, very slowly add about ½ cup of the water. Add the remaining ½ cup water, plus more, if needed, until the sauce reaches the consistency of mayonnaise.

2 Scrape the tahini sauce into a bowl and add more lemon juice or salt, if needed, and the hot pepper sauce.

Tahini

Imported from the Middle East, tahini, made from finely ground and sometimes toasted sesame seeds, is readily available in cans or jars. If the tahini has separated, with a layer of oil on the surface, spoon it into a food processor and process briefly just to homogenize it. Then scrape it back into the jar or container. Refrigerated, tahini seems to keep forever. Do not confuse Middle Eastern tahini with Chinese sesame paste (see page 258), which is thicker and more intensely flavored.

Mango and Mint Summer Rolls with Dipping Sauce

Fresh summer rolls from our local Vietnamese restaurant are a must on a warm summer's day. Although they may look complicated to replicate, they really are quite easy. If you've never worked with brittle rounds of rice paper wrappers, the first time can be a little daunting. Give it a try, following the tips for working with rice paper on page 44. Marinate the tofu overnight or for several hours, whatever is most convenient. A coating of cornstarch adds texture to the tofu, which can either be fried or baked. Once you are ready to assemble the rolls, have all the filling ingredients prepped and ready before softening the rice paper. MAKES 4 SERVINGS

Marinated Tofu

7 or 8 ounces (about ½ block) firm tofu

2 tablespoons soy sauce or tamari (see page 44)

2 tablespoons unseasoned Japanese rice vinegar

1 tablespoon honey

2 teaspoons toasted sesame oil (see page 221)

1 teaspoon chile-garlic sauce or Sriracha, or to taste

Vegetable oil, for frying (optional)

½ cup cornstarch

Dipping Sauce

¼ cup fresh lime juice

¼ cup unseasoned Japanese rice vinegar

1 tablespoon soy sauce or tamari (see page 44)

1 tablespoon sugar

2 teaspoons minced jalapeño pepper, or more to taste

Summer Roll Assembly

4 large soft, curly-leaf lettuce leaves, thick stems trimmed, halved down the middle

2 scallions, cut into 2-inch lengths and then sliced into ⅛-inch-thin julienne pieces (green and white parts)

1 large ripe mango, peeled, pitted, and cut into thin (¼-inch) sticks

½ cup coarsely chopped fresh cilantro leaves

½ cup coarsely chopped fresh mint leaves

8 large rice paper wrappers (see page 44)

1 **Make the tofu:** Cut the tofu into 8 long, thin strips. Place the tofu in a single layer in a shallow dish. In a small bowl, whisk together the soy sauce, vinegar, honey, sesame oil, and chile-garlic sauce until blended. Spoon evenly over the tofu. Refrigerate, covered, for 2 to 3 hours, overnight, or until ready to cook.

2 If frying the tofu, heat the oil in a wide skillet until shimmering or hot enough to brown a crust of bread. Or, if baking, preheat the oven to 400°F and line a baking sheet with parchment paper. Spread the cornstarch on a plate. Lift the tofu strips from the marinade and dredge lightly in the cornstarch. Fry the tofu, turning gently with a spatula as the pieces brown, for about 3 minutes. If baking, place the cornstarch-coated strips of tofu on the lined baking sheet with plenty of room between the pieces. Spoon any marinade left on the plate over the tofu and bake until lightly browned, turning once, about 45 minutes.

3 Make the dipping sauce: In a small bowl, combine the lime juice, vinegar, soy sauce, and sugar; stir to dissolve the sugar. Add the jalapeño and set the sauce aside until ready to serve.

4 Assemble the summer rolls: Have ready the lettuce leaves, scallions, mango, cilantro, and mint assembly-line style on the work counter. Have ready a wide bowl of cold water and a baking sheet lined with a clean kitchen towel. Half fill a large, shallow pot with water and bring to a simmer;

reduce the heat to low. Dip 1 sheet of rice paper into the hot water and let stand until soft and pliable, about 5 *seconds*. Quickly lift it from the hot water with a fork and dip into the bowl of cold water. The wrinkled rice paper will "unwrinkle" when it hits the cold water. Using your fingers, gently lift the rice paper from the cold water and place it on the kitchen towel, gently flattening and spreading it out with your fingertips to its original round shape.

5 Making one summer roll at a time, place a lettuce leaf half on the rice paper, centering it so that there is about 1 inch of rice paper visible at the edges. Lay one tofu strip, 2 or 3 strips of mango, a bit of scallion, and a pinch each of mint and cilantro down the center of the leaf. Fold in about 1 inch from the bottom and the top of the rice paper and then, beginning at the left, tightly roll the rice paper around the filling. Seal the seam against the roll. Place the roll, seam side down, on a platter and cover tightly with plastic wrap or a dampened kitchen towel. Repeat with the remaining rice paper and ingredients until all the rolls are assembled. Serve with the dipping sauce.

Rice Paper Wrappers for Summer Rolls

Rice paper wrappers are sold in Asian markets or the Asian section of well-stocked supermarkets. The printing on the cellophane will be indecipherable but you will recognize them by their almost glasslike appearance. Here are a few pointers for making summer rolls: The rounds of rice paper need to be dipped, one at a time, into very hot water to soften them, which will take about 5 seconds. The rice paper will wrinkle up and look more fragile than it really is. Lift it from the hot water with a fork and dip at once into a bowl of cold water, where it will unwrinkle as it cools, making it easier to handle. Spread the softened rice paper on a kitchen towel to blot off excess water. When filling the roll, don't be tempted to over-stuff it. As the rolls are filled, wrap each in a piece of plastic wrap or cover with a damp towel so it won't dry out and turn tough while you are making the others. If your first few attempts are not successful, discard the torn wrapper, save the fillings, and start again. Practice makes perfect. Any unused rice paper can be slipped into a plastic bag, sealed, and stored in the pantry for what seems like forever.

Soy Sauce or Tamari

Soy sauce and tamari are both made from soybeans, but tamari is thicker, smoother, and richer. Typically tamari does not include wheat. Soy sauce contains wheat and has a saltier flavor. They can be used interchangeably, but, if I have a choice, I prefer tamari.

Arancini with Mushrooms, Peas, and Cheese

A trip to Sicily many years ago brought me to Vucciria, the well-known open-air market in Palermo, where I stuffed myself with arancini, fried rice balls. True to their name, which means "little oranges" in Italian, those arancini were as big as oranges. They were also orange in color from the addition of saffron. They can be filled with a mixture of meat and cheese, or with vegetables and cheese, as here. My recipe makes much smaller balls, more like Key limes than oranges. Because they are labor-intensive, I recommend making them ahead. They can even be fried and refrigerated or frozen, and then reheated in a hot oven. MAKES 12

Rice

2½ cups Roasted Vegetable Broth (page 120) or half broth and half water

½ teaspoon crumbled saffron threads

3 tablespoons extra-virgin olive oil

¼ cup finely chopped onion

1 small garlic clove, grated

1 cup Arborio rice

½ cup grated Parmigiano-Reggiano

2 large egg yolks, whites reserved for the coating

Filling

8 ounces exotic mushrooms, such as cremini, shiitake, oyster, matsutake, or hedgehog

2 tablespoons extra-virgin olive oil

1 small garlic clove, grated

½ teaspoon coarse salt

Freshly ground black pepper

½ cup frozen petite peas, thawed

1 cup (about 4 ounces) finely shredded Fontina, Montasio, or other flavorful melting cheese, preferably Italian

1 cup all-purpose flour

2 cups fine dry bread crumbs

Vegetable oil, for frying

1 **Make the rice:** In a small saucepan, bring the broth and saffron to a boil. Reduce the heat, cover, and keep hot until ready to cook the risotto.

2 Combine the oil and onion in a large wide saucepan over medium-low heat and cook, stirring, until the onion begins to sizzle. Reduce the heat to low and cook, stirring, until the onion is translucent but not brown, about 5 minutes. Stir in the garlic and remove from the heat. Add the rice and stir to coat with the oil. Stir in the

saffron-infused broth and bring to a boil over high heat. Stir well, cover, and cook over medium-low heat until the broth is absorbed and the rice is soft, about 20 minutes. Remove from the heat, stir in the Parmigiano-Reggiano, and let stand until cooled.

3 Stir the egg yolks into the cooled rice until well blended. Lightly oil a 13-x-9-inch baking pan and spread the rice in the pan. Place a sheet of plastic wrap directly on the rice. Refrigerate until cold and ready to shape, about 30 minutes.

4 Meanwhile, make the filling: Remove and discard the stems from the shiitake mushrooms, if using. Finely chop all of the mushrooms, caps and tender stems included. You will have about 2 cups. Heat the oil in a large skillet until hot enough to sizzle a piece of mushroom. Add the mushrooms and cook, stirring, over medium to medium-high heat until the mushrooms are tender and free of moisture, about 10 minutes. Remove from the heat. Stir in the garlic, salt, and a generous grinding of black pepper. Stir in the peas and set aside until cooled. Once cool, stir in the cheese. (The filling can be made ahead and refrigerated for 1 to 2 days.)

5 When ready to shape the arancini, beat the egg whites in a shallow bowl until foamy. Place the flour and the bread crumbs on two separate plates or sheets of wax paper. Have ready a baking sheet. Use a knife to cut the rice into 12 evenly sized squares. Wet your hands with cold water. Place a square of rice in the palm of your hand. Flatten the rice in your palm and place a rounded tablespoon of the filling mixture in the center. Gently close your hand so that the rice surrounds the filling. Smooth the outside to form a ball. Repeat with the remaining rice, wetting your hands often to prevent the rice from sticking to them.

6 Coat all the filled rice balls lightly with the flour. Hold the floured rice ball in your hand with your fingers spread and gently shake off any excess flour. When all the rice balls are coated with flour, dip them in the egg whites, letting the excess drip off. Roll in the bread crumbs until evenly coated. Arrange on a tray as you coat each ball. Refrigerate for 30 minutes so they can set and dry out a bit. (The balls can be made one day ahead and refrigerated until ready to fry.)

7 To fry the arancini, heat about 3 inches of vegetable oil in a deep, wide saucepan until hot enough to brown a crust of bread, or about 350°F on a deep-frying thermometer. Fry a few arancini at a time, gently turning with a skimmer or slotted spoon, until they turn a deep golden brown, 5 to 10 minutes. Transfer the arancini to a wire rack or a plate lined with a double thickness of paper towels to drain as you finish each batch. Serve warm or at room temperature. To reheat refrigerated or frozen fried arancini, bake in a preheated 350°F oven until heated through, about 20 minutes.

BREADS AND SANDWICHES

Irish Brown Bread, page 51

Irish Brown Bread

I enjoyed a version of this brown bread many years ago on a trip to Ireland, and I've been making it ever since. The unusual blend of almond meal, whole-wheat pastry flour, buttermilk, and yogurt lends an especially tender texture and rich taste. It is excellent smeared with butter, jam, or a drizzle of honey. **MAKES ONE 8- OR 9-INCH ROUND LOAF**

2 cups buttermilk

1 large egg

½ cup plain low-fat yogurt, preferably Greek style

5 tablespoons unsalted butter, melted

2 tablespoons honey

2 teaspoons grated lemon zest

2½ cups whole-wheat pastry flour

2 cups all-purpose flour

2 teaspoons baking soda

1 teaspoon coarse salt

½ cup almond meal

½ cup finely chopped skin-on (natural) almonds

1 Preheat the oven to 350°F. Lightly butter the bottom and sides of an 8- or 9-inch springform pan.

2 In a bowl, whisk together the buttermilk, egg, yogurt, 4 tablespoons of the melted butter, the honey, and lemon zest until thoroughly blended.

3 In a large bowl, stir together the whole-wheat flour, all-purpose flour, baking soda, and salt until blended. Stir in the almond meal and almonds. Add the buttermilk mixture and gently fold just to moisten all the ingredients. Spoon into the prepared pan. Drizzle the remaining 1 tablespoon melted butter over the top.

4 Bake until the sides have pulled away from the pan and the top is crisp and golden, 1 hour and 20 to 30 minutes. Let cool thoroughly. Run a knife around the edges of the pan and unlatch the springform. Slide the bread onto a cutting board and halve down the middle. Place cut side down and slice each half into ½-inch-thick slices. Extra bread freezes very well.

Cornmeal Spoonbread

This classic Southern casserole combines stovetop-stirred corn grits with eggs, scallions, and cheese to make a soft, fragrant, appealingly moist bread that must be served with a spoon. **MAKES 4 SERVINGS**

1 cup grits (yellow or white)

1 teaspoon coarse salt

3 cups water

3 tablespoons unsalted butter

1 teaspoon grated garlic (2 or 3 cloves)

¾ cup fresh, canned, or thawed frozen corn kernels

¼ cup chopped scallion (green and white parts)

2 large eggs

Whole milk, as needed

1 tablespoon Tabasco or other hot sauce, or more to taste

2 cups shredded sharp cheddar cheese

1 Preheat the oven to 350°F. Lightly butter the bottom and sides of a 2½-quart casserole or baking dish.

2 Combine the grits, salt, and water in a medium saucepan and bring to a boil. Cook, stirring constantly, until the cornmeal thickens, about 5 minutes. Transfer to a large bowl and stir until slightly cooled.

3 Meanwhile, melt the butter in a small saucepan. Add the garlic and cook, stirring, over low heat until the garlic sizzles and the butter foams. Remove from the heat. Stir in the corn and scallions and set aside.

4 Break the eggs into a measuring cup and add enough milk to measure 1 cup. Lightly whisk together the eggs and milk. Stir in the hot sauce.

5 Fold 1 cup of the cheese and the corn mixture into the partially cooled grits. Add the egg mixture and fold together until thoroughly blended.

6 Pour into the buttered baking dish and sprinkle the remaining 1 cup cheese on top. Bake until browned and puffed, 45 to 50 minutes. Serve hot.

Za'atar Flatbread

Za'atar, the Middle Eastern spice blend that usually includes dried thyme, marjoram, oregano, ground sumac, and sesame seeds, is often blended with olive oil and served drizzled over bread or vegetables. In this recipe, it is liberally sprinkled on well-oiled dough before baking. You can also sprinkle it on store-bought naan, spongy-type pita rounds (not the pocket type), or slices of Crostini (page 23). It has a delicious, pungent taste.

MAKES 4 SERVINGS

1 pound pizza dough, store-bought or homemade (recipe follows)

Yellow cornmeal, as needed

Extra-virgin olive oil, as needed

4 teaspoons za'atar (see page 32)

1 Punch down the pizza dough if it has risen and divide the dough into 4 portions. On a floured surface, flatten each portion with the heel of your hand and then let stand, covered, for about 15 minutes. Then, with floured hands, gently stretch each portion of dough from the outside edges into an oval about 7 inches long and 4 inches wide.

2 Sprinkle one large or two smaller baking sheets with cornmeal. Liberally brush the surface of the pizza ovals with olive oil on both sides and place on the baking sheet or sheets. Sprinkle each with about 1 teaspoon of the za'atar, cover with a towel, and let stand for about 30 minutes.

3 Arrange the oven racks in the lower half of the oven and preheat to 400°F.

4 Bake the flatbreads until lightly browned on the bottom, about 10 minutes. Remove the baking sheet from the oven and carefully turn over the flatbreads. Return to the oven and bake until browned on the other side, about 5 minutes more. Let cool slightly.

5 Transfer to a cutting board and cut crosswise into 1-inch-wide pieces to serve.

Variation
TOMATO AND ZA'ATAR FLATBREAD

Prepare the flatbread according to the recipe above, but in step 2, top each flatbread with 4 or 5 thinly sliced rounds of plum tomato before sprinkling with the za'atar. Bake, without turning the breads, until the bottoms are browned and the surfaces golden, 12 to 15 minutes.

Pizza Dough

**MAKES ENOUGH FOR 4 SMALL
(6- TO 8-INCH) PIZZAS**

- ¼ cup warm (105° to 115°F) water plus 1 cup room-temperature water
- 2 teaspoons active dry yeast
- 1 teaspoon honey or sugar
- 2 tablespoons extra-virgin olive oil
- 2 teaspoons coarse salt
- 3½ to 4 cups all-purpose flour, plus more as needed

1 Combine the ¼ cup warm water with the yeast and honey in a large bowl; stir to blend. Cover with plastic wrap and let stand for about 10 minutes, or until foamy.

2 Mix in the remaining 1 cup water, the oil, salt, and 1½ cups of the flour and stir until smooth. Gradually add the remaining 2 to 2½ cups flour, stirring until the dough comes away from the sides of the bowl.

3 Turn the dough out onto a floured surface and knead by hand for about 10 minutes, or until the dough is smooth and elastic, adding as much extra flour as needed to keep the dough from being too sticky. Alternatively, knead the dough with a dough hook using a stand mixer for about 5 minutes. The dough is adequately kneaded when it springs back when poked lightly with a fingertip.

4 Shape the dough into a ball and place it in a large, oiled bowl. Turn the dough to coat with the oil. Cover the bowl with plastic wrap and let the dough rise in a warm place for about 1 hour, or until doubled in bulk.

5 Punch down the dough and divide and shape as directed in the recipe. If not using the dough right away, punch it down, cover lightly with plastic wrap, and refrigerate for up to 24 hours. If refrigerated, let the dough stand at room temperature for about 15 minutes before shaping it.

Egg Toast

Early one morning while wandering around New Delhi, India, I watched workers buying sliced white bread that had been dipped in beaten eggs and fried. It's a preparation reminiscent—except for the savory spices and herbs—of French toast. On the streets of Delhi, the bread is folded in half and wrapped in paper to eat on the way to work or to save for a mid-morning snack. Back in my home kitchen, I stand at the stove and fry my egg bread in a shallow pool of hot ghee. MAKES 1 SERVING

¼ cup cumin seeds or ½ teaspoon toasted cumin seeds

1 large egg, plus a second egg (optional)

2 tablespoons milk or water

½ teaspoon Madras curry powder (see page 279)

¼ teaspoon minced fresh hot red pepper or serrano chile, or more to taste

Pinch of coarse salt

1 slice firm white bread

1 tablespoon ghee (see page 76) or vegetable oil

1 tablespoon finely chopped fresh cilantro

1 If you don't have a supply of toasted cumin seeds on hand, spread the ¼ cup cumin seeds in a small skillet set over medium heat. Shake the pan on the heat until the seeds begin to change color and are fragrant, about 3 minutes. Let cool. You will need ½ teaspoon for the egg toast; transfer the remaining to a jar for future use.

2 In a shallow bowl, whisk 1 egg, the milk, curry powder, toasted cumin seeds, hot red pepper, and salt. Add the bread and press down lightly with the back of a fork to soak in the egg. Let stand for 5 minutes. Turn and soak the other side, pressing lightly, until all the egg is absorbed, about 5 minutes.

3 Heat a small skillet over medium-high heat until hot enough to sizzle a drop of water. Add the ghee and heat until hot enough to sizzle the egg-soaked bread. Add the bread, scraping any seasonings left in the bowl onto the surface. Adjust the temperature to medium and cook until browned on the bottom, about 5 minutes. Flip the bread. If using the second egg, break it into a bowl. Make a slight indentation in the toast with the back of a spoon and slide the egg into the indentation. Cover and cook until the egg is cooked to the desired doneness, about 3 minutes for a medium-runny yolk. If not using the second egg, cook until the other side of the toast is lightly browned.

4 Sprinkle with the cilantro and enjoy.

Scallion Pancakes with Spicy Dipping Sauce

This scallion pancake is adapted from *The Key to Chinese Cooking* by Irene Kuo, a cookbook well used in my kitchen for many years that is now, sadly, out of print. The batter goes together quickly and the pancakes are cooked in a matter of minutes. They are aromatic with scallion and just oily enough to be authentic. The sesame seeds add an irresistible crunch and great taste. I serve scallion pancakes, torn into pieces, in a bread basket with soup or with a vegetable stir-fry. The Spicy Dipping Sauce is a nice touch if you are serving the basket of scallion pancakes with a cool drink before supper. **MAKES 4 PANCAKES**

1 cup all-purpose flour

½ teaspoon coarse salt

¾ cup water, plus more as needed

1 large egg, beaten

2 teaspoons toasted sesame oil (see page 221)

½ cup finely chopped scallion (white and green parts)

1 tablespoon vegetable oil, plus more as needed

2 teaspoons toasted sesame seeds (see page 60)

Spicy Dipping Sauce, for serving (optional; recipe follows)

1 Combine the flour and the salt in a medium bowl. In a separate bowl, beat together the water, egg, and sesame oil until blended. Gradually add the egg mixture to the flour, stirring with a fork until the batter is smooth. It should be the consistency of heavy cream. If it is too thick, add more water, ½ tablespoon at a time. Stir in the scallions.

2 Heat a small (7- to 8-inch) heavy skillet with gently sloping sides until hot enough to sizzle a drop of water. Add the vegetable oil and swirl the pan to evenly coat the surface. Over medium-low heat, add a scant ⅓ cup of the batter with one hand while tipping and turning the pan with your other hand so the batter covers the surface to make a thin pancake. Sprinkle the surface with about ½ teaspoon of the sesame seeds.

3 Cook over medium to medium-low heat until the bottom is lightly browned and the top appears set, about 2 minutes. Carefully turn the pancake with a wide rubber spatula and cook the other side, about 2 minutes.

continued >

4 Repeat with the remaining batter, adding more oil, 1 teaspoon at a time, as needed. Serve hot with the dipping sauce, if desired. Leftovers can be reheated on a baking sheet in a 350°F for 10 minutes.

Spicy Dipping Sauce

⅓ cup soy sauce or tamari (see page 44)

2 tablespoons Chinese black vinegar (see page 114) or balsamic vinegar

2 tablespoons cold water

¼ teaspoon chile oil (see box)

....

In a small bowl, combine the soy sauce, vinegar, cold water, and chile oil. Set aside until ready to serve.

Sesame Seeds

Sesame seeds, native to Africa, come in a variety of colors. I look for sesame seeds in my Asian market, where they come in a tall jar that holds about 12 ounces. The jars of sesame seeds are available as both tan and black. The tan and the black have not been "hulled," so they are sturdier and contribute more texture and have a nutty flavor. The ivory white sesame seeds available in small jars in the spice section in the supermarket have had their hulls removed. Add texture and taste to white sesame seeds by toasting in a skillet, stirring, over low heat 1 to 2 minutes until golden. Store sesame seeds in the freezer or refrigerator, as they are high in fat and will eventually become rancid.

Chile Oil

Chile oil is found in the Asian section of most supermarkets. It is vegetable oil that has been infused with chile peppers. A drop or two will add a major kick of heat to soups, salads, dressings, dips, and rice and noodle dishes. Sometimes toasted sesame oil is infused with chiles, which is a different product but highly flavorful and just as spicy.

Spanakopita with Spinach, Herbs, and Feta

In this recipe, the spanakopita is made in a large pan and cut into portions rather than as individual handheld "spinach pies." For many years I melted sticks of butter and carefully brushed it on the filo, but no longer. I have since learned that olive oil makes the pastry even crisper. Fresh mint, dill, and lemon zest add a bright, fresh taste to the spinach and feta, while sautéed mushrooms add umami. MAKES 6 TO 12 SERVINGS

¾ cup (approximately) extra-virgin olive oil

1½ cups (about 2 bunches) finely sliced scallion (green and white parts)

2 to 3 pounds whole-leaf (not baby) spinach (or a mixture of kale, Swiss chard, and spinach), stems trimmed, rinsed, dried, and coarsely chopped (about 8 cups tightly packed)

¼ cup finely chopped fresh flat-leaf (Italian) parsley

¼ cup finely chopped fresh dill

2 tablespoons finely chopped fresh mint leaves

Coarse salt

¼ teaspoon freshly ground black pepper, plus more for the spinach and mushrooms

4 ounces mixed mushrooms, such as shiitake, cremini, and/or oyster, tough stems trimmed from shiitake, coarsely chopped

1 garlic clove, finely chopped

2 large eggs

1½ cups (about 4 ounces) crumbled feta (see page 62), preferably Greek or French

2 tablespoons grated Pecorino Romano

2 teaspoons grated lemon zest

¼ teaspoon grated nutmeg

12 large sheets thawed filo

1 Warm 2 tablespoons of the oil in a large, deep skillet with a lid over medium-low heat. Add the scallions and cook, stirring, until almost tender, about 5 minutes. Add the spinach, still damp from rinsing, cover, and cook until wilted, about 5 minutes. Uncover and continue to cook, stirring, to evaporate any excess moisture from the greens. Spoon into a strainer set over a bowl and press down with the back of a spoon to extract as much liquid as possible. Transfer to a large bowl and add the parsley, dill, mint, a pinch of salt, and a grinding of pepper. Let cool.

2 Wipe out the skillet, add 2 tablespoons oil, and heat until hot enough to sizzle a piece of mushroom. Add the mushrooms and cook, stirring, until the mushrooms are tender and any juices have evaporated,

about 10 minutes. Stir in the garlic and cook for about 30 seconds. Season with a pinch of salt and a grinding of pepper.

3 In a large bowl, beat the eggs until well blended. Stir in the feta, Pecorino Romano, lemon zest, the ¼ teaspoon pepper, and the nutmeg. Add the spinach and herb mixture and the mushrooms and stir to combine.

4 Preheat the oven to 350°F. Lightly oil a 13-x-9-inch baking pan. Halve the large sheets of filo to make twenty-four 13-x-9-inch sheets. One sheet at a time, place 12 sheets on the bottom of the pan, lightly brushing each with some of the remaining ½ cup olive oil. Spread the egg and spinach mixture in an even layer. One at a time, top with the remaining 12 sheets filo, brushing each one lightly with the oil.

5 With a sharp knife, cut through the layers to make 3 squares across and 4 down for 12 portions. If preferred, you can cut each square in half diagonally to make smaller triangular portions. Brush the top of the spanakopita lightly with olive oil.

6 Bake until the top of the spanakopita is puffed and browned, about 60 minutes. Let cool. Cut down through the indentations and remove the pieces individually from the pan with a small spatula.

The World of Feta Cheese

Ideally you should purchase feta from a shop where the cheese is stored in tubs of brine and you can taste the various types before deciding which you like best. But increasingly, feta is sold shrink-wrapped in packages. Here are some guidelines to help you choose:

Greek Feta Considered by many to be the benchmark by which all feta is judged, it is typically a combination of sheep and goat's milks, although cow's milk is sometimes used. The blend of milks contributes to the sweet-salty-sour flavor notes, with the high-fat sheep's milk adding creaminess.

French Feta Made from the excess sheep's milk left over from the production of Roquefort, French feta is a mild cheese, less salty than Greek feta, with a creamy mouthfeel. I prefer this variety.

Israeli Feta Made primarily with goat's milk, this feta has a flavor and texture that fall somewhere between the Greek and the French styles.

Bulgarian Feta This feta has a salty, bold taste and a dry, crumbly texture.

Domestic Feta More and more local artisanal cheesemakers are producing excellent feta cheese. Look for domestic goat's-milk feta at your local farmers' market or in a well-stocked cheese department of your local cheese shop or supermarket.

Winter Squash and Mushroom Empanada Grande

This olive oil dough is amazingly supple and easy to use and also wonderfully tender and flaky. I'd like to claim credit for both the concept of an empanada made in a baking pan and the pastry recipe, but both are from my friend and neighbor, Barbara May, a retired Spanish language professor. The stuffing of winter squash, greens, mushrooms, and Manchego cheese laced with smoked paprika is my contribution. MAKES 6 TO 8 SERVINGS

Olive Oil Pastry

2½ cups all-purpose flour

½ teaspoon coarse salt

½ cup extra-virgin olive oil

⅓ cup water, plus more as needed

Filling and Assembly

2 cups peeled, seeded, and cubed (½-inch pieces) dense winter squash, preferably butternut or kabocha (about 12 ounces)

4 cups lightly packed Tuscan kale, Swiss chard, spinach, or a combination of winter greens, chopped (tough stems removed if necessary)

3 tablespoons extra-virgin olive oil

2½ cups (about 8 ounces) chopped cremini or white button mushrooms

½ cup chopped onion

1 garlic clove, grated

1 teaspoon smoked paprika, preferably pimentón de la Vera (see page 26)

½ teaspoon coarse salt, or more to taste

Freshly ground black pepper

½ cup (about 2 ounces) coarsely grated Manchego cheese (see page 65)

2 to 3 teaspoons minced jalapeño pepper, or to taste

1 large egg, beaten

1 Make the pastry: Combine the flour and salt in a food processor and pulse to blend. Gradually add the oil while continuously pulsing until blended. Slowly add the water through the feed tube, continuing to pulse until the dough clumps and forms a soft ball. If the mixture is dry, add more water, 1 tablespoon at a time, pulsing after each addition. The dough should be soft to the touch.

2 Remove the blade and, with floured hands, gather the dough into a ball and place on a lightly floured surface. Gently knead the dough for about 30 seconds, or just long enough to form a smooth ball. Do not overwork the dough or it will become tough. Cover with plastic wrap and refrigerate until ready to roll.

3 Make the filling: Place the squash in a steamer basket and place over boiling water. Steam, covered, until very tender, 10 to 15 minutes depending on the type of squash. Remove the squash to a bowl.

4 Place the greens in the steamer, and steam, covered, until wilted and tender, 5 to 15 minutes depending on the toughness of the leaves. Remove the steamer, set over a plate, and press down on the greens to squeeze out some of the moisture. Place the greens on a kitchen towel and press to remove all of the moisture. You should have about ½ cup.

5 Heat the oil in a large skillet until hot enough to sizzle a piece of the onion. Add the mushrooms and onions and cook, stirring, over medium heat until the mushrooms and onions turn golden, 10 to 12 minutes. Add the garlic, smoked paprika, salt, and a generous grinding of black pepper. Cook, stirring, for about 1 minute. Remove from the heat.

6 Mash the cooked squash with a fork or a potato masher and add to the mushroom mixture. Add the greens, cheese, and jalapeño. Stir to blend. Taste and add more salt, if needed.

7 Preheat the oven to 350°F. Spray a 13-x-9-inch baking pan with nonstick spray. Divide the dough in half and, with a rolling pin, gently roll one half of the dough to fit into the pan with about ¼ inch extra on each side. Transfer the dough to the pan and with floured fingers coax the dough to the edges and slightly up the sides.

8 Spread the filling in the pastry-lined pan. Roll out the remaining dough and place it on top of the filling. Fold the bottom edges over the top layer of pastry and pinch with fingertips to seal. Beat the egg until frothy and brush on top of the dough. With the tip of a knife or a fork, pierce the dough at 1-inch intervals.

9 Bake until golden, 45 to 50 minutes. Let cool slightly. Cut into 12 or 16 evenly sized squares or rectangles. (Larger pieces can be cut into triangles.) Serve warm or at room temperature. Leftover refrigerated empanada will reheat in a 350°F oven in 10 to 15 minutes.

Manchego Cheese

Manchego, or queso Manchego, is a popular Spanish sheep's-milk cheese now readily available at well-stocked cheese counters in many supermarkets. It is firm enough to be shredded and has a creamy, nutty, not too salty—or sharp—taste. I like it for its pleasing melting properties. (It makes a killer grilled cheese sandwich.) It is a great cheese to keep on hand. Cut into small squares, and paired with membrillo (Spanish quince paste), it makes a quick snack or simple appetizer. Substitute an aged dry Jack cheese from California, if preferred.

Roasted Poblano, Egg, and Tomato Empanada Grande with Feta

The tomato and hard-cooked-egg filling in this filled flaky pastry made in a baking pan is spicy and fresh and perfectly balanced, with richness from the eggs and tangy and salty from the crumbled feta and green olives.

MAKES 6 TO 8 SERVINGS

2 or 3 medium poblano chiles (8 to 10 ounces)

2 tablespoons extra-virgin olive oil

¾ cup chopped onion

1½ teaspoons ground cumin

1 teaspoon chile powder

1 can (14.5 ounces) diced tomatoes with their juices

3 hard-cooked eggs, peeled and coarsely chopped

½ cup crumbled feta cheese (about 4 ounces; see page 62)

⅓ cup chopped pimiento-stuffed green olives

2 tablespoons chopped fresh cilantro

1 tablespoon minced jalapeño pepper

Coarse salt

1 recipe Olive Oil Pastry (page 64)

1 large egg, beaten

1 Preheat the broiler. Line a baking sheet with foil and place the poblano chiles on the foil. Place the baking sheet on the shelf about 2 to 3 inches from the heat source and broil, turning the chiles as they blister and char, about 5 minutes. Remove from the broiler, wrap in the foil, and let cool. Once cool enough to handle, unwrap and rub off the charred skins. Split the chiles in half. Remove and discard the stems and seeds and coarsely chop the chiles.

2 Heat the oil in a skillet over medium heat until hot enough to sizzle a piece of onion. Add the onion and cook, stirring, over medium-low heat until softened, about 10 minutes. Add the cumin and chile powder and cook, stirring, for about 1 minute.

3 Add the tomatoes and bring to a boil. Adjust the heat and boil, uncovered, until the sauce is very thick and mounds when stirred with a spoon, 12 to 15 minutes. Remove from the heat. Add the poblano chiles, hard-cooked eggs, feta, olives, cilantro, and jalapeño; fold gently until combined. Taste and add salt, if needed.

4 Preheat the oven to 350°F. Spray a 13-x-9-inch baking pan with nonstick spray. Divide the dough in half and, with a rolling pin, gently roll one half of the dough to fit into the pan with about ¼ inch extra on each side. Transfer the dough to the pan and with floured fingers coax the dough to the edges and slightly up the sides.

5 Spread the filling in the pastry-lined pan. Roll out the remaining dough and place it on top of the filling. Fold the bottom edges over the top layer of pastry and pinch with your fingertips to seal. Beat the egg until frothy and brush on top of the dough. With the tip of a knife or a fork, pierce the dough at 1-inch intervals.

6 Bake until golden, 45 to 50 minutes. Let cool slightly. Cut into 12 or 16 evenly sized squares or rectangles. (Larger pieces can be cut into triangles.) Serve warm or at room temperature. Leftover refrigerated empanada will reheat in a 350°F oven in 10 to 15 minutes.

Pupusas

Pupusas are a popular street food in El Salvador, and we're lucky to have a pupusa food cart just a few blocks from our home here in Oregon. In El Salvador, these fried patties made of corn flour are filled with all types of ingredients from meat to beans to shredded cheese. At the cart I frequent, Juanita's Pupusas, Juanita fills hers with what she calls Mexican mozzarella, which I find at my local Latin American market labeled as queso asadero (see page 249). They are almost always served with a thinly sliced cabbage slaw seasoned with white vinegar, oregano, and salt. MAKES 8

2 cups masa harina (see page 70)

1 teaspoon coarse salt

3 tablespoons vegetable oil, plus more for frying

1 to 2 cups very hot water

½ cup shredded queso asadero (see page 249) or Monterey Jack cheese

Pickled Cabbage Slaw (page 125), for serving

1 Stir together the masa harina and salt in a medium bowl until blended. Drizzle with the oil and work with your fingertips or a table fork until blended. Gradually add the water, while tossing with your fingers or a fork, adding just enough so that the dough pulls away from the sides of the bowl and comes together in a ball. The dough should be very soft.

2 Turn the dough out onto a lightly floured work surface and lightly knead until smooth, about 2 minutes. Cover with a bowl and let the dough rest for 1 to 2 hours.

3 Divide the dough in half and shape into two ropes about 4 inches long. Cut each rope into 1-inch pieces. Shape each piece into a ball and set aside on a tray or along one side of your work surface. Cover with a damp kitchen towel.

4 With lightly oiled hands, pat 1 ball at a time into a fat patty. Holding the patty in one cupped hand, shape the patty to match the form of your hand so that there is an indentation in the center. Place a generous pinch (about 1 tablespoon) of cheese in the indentation. Close your hand around the cheese to cover. Pat the filled patty between your hands until flattened to about ½ inch thick. It's all right if the cheese leaks out a little bit because it'll turn brown and

crusty as the pupusas cook. Repeat with the remaining dough.

5 In a heavy skillet, heat ¼ inch of oil until hot enough to sizzle a pinch of dough. Add the pupusas and cook over medium to medium-high heat until lightly browned, about 4 minutes per side. Serve warm, accompanied by the Pickled Cabbage Slaw.

Masa Harina

Pupusas are made with masa harina, or corn flour, the same flour used to make tortillas. This corn flour is made from specially treated corn before being ground and is not interchangeable with cornmeal. Latin markets and most well-stocked supermarkets carry masa harina.

Kimchi Quesadillas

Kimchi quesadillas are a surprisingly delicious creation. This unlikely combination consists of kimchi (my own recipe), a generous layer of Monterey Jack cheese, and slivered green cabbage, folded into a flour tortilla and toasted until the cheese turns oozy. **MAKES 2 SERVINGS**

2 large (8-inch) flour tortillas

Extra-virgin olive oil, as needed

1 cup chopped Vegetarian Kimchi (page 133)

6 ounces Monterey Jack or mozzarella cheese, cut into ⅛-inch-thick slivers or coarsely shredded (about 1 cup)

1½ cups finely shredded green cabbage

1 Preheat the oven to 400°F. Brush one side of each tortilla with a thin film of oil and place oiled side down on a baking sheet.

2 Spread half of each tortilla with the kimchi. Top with a layer of cheese, then spread the cabbage on top of the cheese. Fold the tortilla onto the cabbage layer to make 2 half circles. Brush the tops of the quesadillas with more oil.

3 Bake until the bottoms are browned and the cheese is melted, about 15 minutes. With a large, wide spatula, flip the quesadillas and bake just until the bottoms are golden, about 5 minutes more. Cool slightly, then cut each quesadilla into 3 or 4 pie-shaped wedges.

Feta, Black Olive, and Harissa–Stuffed Brik

In Tunisian *brik*, squares of very thin pastry called *ouark* are filled sometimes with greens or meat, folded into triangles, fried, and eaten out of hand. Chinese egg roll wrappers make the best substitute for the traditional pastry. This version is stuffed with feta cheese, black olives, cilantro, and a bit of harissa, a hot pepper condiment. **MAKES 8 TO 12; 2 TO 6 SERVINGS**

⅔ cup (about 4 ounces) crumbled feta cheese (see page 62)

¼ cup chopped pitted kalamata olives

1 tablespoon harissa (see box), or to taste

1 tablespoon finely chopped fresh cilantro

8 to 12 fresh or thawed frozen 3-inch square Chinese egg roll wrappers

1 large egg white

Vegetable oil, for frying

1 Line up the feta, olives, harissa, and cilantro in an assembly line on your work counter. Separate the egg roll wrappers and place them on a work surface, covered with dampened paper towels. Whisk the egg white in a small bowl until foamy. Have ready a pastry brush.

2 In the center of each egg roll wrapper, place 1 rounded tablespoon of feta, ½ tablespoon of olives, ¼ teaspoon of harissa, and a pinch of cilantro. Brush the edges of the wrapper with the egg white. Fold into a triangle and press the edges to seal. If they don't stick, reapply the egg white.

3 Have ready a wire rack set over a baking sheet. Heat ¼ inch of oil in a medium skillet until hot enough to sizzle a bread crust. Fry 3 or 4 *brik* at a time, turning gently with a slotted spoon, until lightly browned, adjusting the heat to keep them from browning too quickly, about 2 minutes per side.

4 With a slotted spoon or a wire skimmer remove the *brik* from the hot oil to the wire rack as you finish each batch. Serve hot.

Harissa

Harissa is a thick Tunisian hot sauce made with chiles, garlic, caraway, and other spices. It is made in home kitchens, but is also readily available in both Middle Eastern and specialty markets in jars, cans, or tubes. Taste before adding it to dishes to test its heat, for some are hotter than others. In a pinch, crushed red pepper flakes can be substituted, but it won't have the nuanced flavors in harissa.

Chapatis

Chapatis (also called roti) are small round disks of unleavened whole-grain bread cooked on a skillet, griddle, or grill. Chapati flour is available in many Middle Eastern grocery or health food stores, but if it is unavailable, make the breads (as I do) with equal parts all-purpose white flour and whole-wheat flour. Chapatis are always served warm and brushed with clarified butter, ghee, or plain melted butter. **MAKES 12; 4 TO 6 SERVINGS**

2 cups chapati flour (see page 76) or
   1 cup unbleached all-purpose flour plus
   1 cup whole-wheat flour

1 teaspoon coarse salt

¾ cup warm water

4 tablespoons clarified butter (ghee; see
   page 76), or melted butter

1 Place the flour in a large bowl and add the salt. If using two different flours, stir with a wooden spoon until blended. Gradually add the water and 1 tablespoon of the butter, stirring with a wooden spoon until the dough comes together into a sticky ball. Transfer the dough to a lightly floured board and knead until smooth, about 3 minutes. Invert the bowl over the dough and let stand for about 20 minutes.

2 Divide the dough equally into 12 pieces. With floured hands, form each piece of dough into a ball. Press the ball into a disk about ½ inch thick and use a rolling pin to roll each disk on a lightly floured board into a circle about 3 inches in diameter. As the circles are rolled, set them aside without touching and cover with a kitchen towel so they won't dry out.

3 Keep the remaining butter warm in a small saucepan over low heat. Have ready two large sheets of foil. Place one on a large tray or baking sheet.

4 Heat a large heavy skillet (cast iron works well) over medium to medium-high heat until hot enough to sizzle and evaporate a drop of water upon contact. Cook the breads 1 or 2 at a time until brown spots appear on the underside, 2 to 3 minutes. Turn with tongs and cook for about 2 minutes longer. The breads will puff up. Place on the foil-lined tray and brush with the warm butter. Cover with the second sheet of foil to keep warm. Repeat with the remaining dough.

Ghee

Ghee is basically Indian-style clarified butter. To clarify butter, slowly heat until melted. As it melts, the milk solids will sink to the bottom of the pan and foam will rise to the top. The clear yellow liquid is strained and is called clarified butter. For ghee the process is the same, but the white solids are sometimes lightly browned, adding a nutty taste to the ghee. Removing the milk solids raises the smoking point, which means ghee can be used for frying without fear of burning. Ghee is sold in jars in many supermarkets, or you can make it yourself at home. Ghee imported from India is expensive but it has a slightly different flavor due to the grazing land for Indian cows, or water buffalo. Ghee is kept at room temperature without fear of spoiling.

Chapati Flour

Chapati flour is a blend of wheat and barley flours sold in Indian markets labeled as *atta*, or flour. A combination of whole-wheat flour and all-purpose flour is an acceptable substitute.

Vegetable Torta with Eggs, Beans, and Cactus Salad

Along my regular bike route I pass a tiny food cart called Xoco. The two young proprietors make delicious Mexican food to take out, including this *torta,* or Mexican sandwich. Their vegetarian version contains a thin egg omelet, mashed avocado, shredded lettuce, thin-sliced marinated onion, a not-too-thick layer of cactus salad, and a layer of smashed pinto beans pressed into the bottom half of the roll. The rolls, or *bolillos,* are oval-shaped sandwich rolls about 6 inches long with a crusty outside and soft inside. Almost any roll by that description can be used, unless you are fortunate to have a Mexican bakery nearby. Most of the parts of the sandwich—the cactus salad, pinto beans, and vinegar onions—can be made a day or two ahead and refrigerated so they are at the ready for assembling the sandwich. MAKES 2 SERVINGS

3 tablespoons plus 1 teaspoon extra-virgin olive oil

¼ cup finely chopped onion, plus ½ cup paper-thin half slices

1 garlic clove, grated

1 can (15 ounces) pinto beans or 1½ cups cooked dried pinto beans, well drained

½ teaspoon Mexican oregano (see page 110)

Coarse salt and freshly ground black pepper

2 large eggs

1 tablespoon water

1 tablespoon white vinegar

2 Mexican bolillos, or oval crusty rolls with a soft interior, split lengthwise

Cactus Salad (page 159)

½ cup lightly packed shredded curly-leaf lettuce

½ ripe avocado, peeled, pitted, and cut into small chunks

Hot sauce (optional)

1 Heat 3 tablespoons of the oil in a medium skillet until hot enough to sizzle a pinch of onion. Add the chopped onion and cook, stirring occasionally, over medium-low heat, until the onions are golden brown, about 5 minutes. Add the garlic and cook, stirring, for about 10 seconds. Add the beans, oregano, a pinch of salt, and a generous grinding of black pepper and cook, mashing the beans with a table fork

until partially mashed, for about 2 minutes. Set aside.

2 Whisk together the eggs and water in a small bowl until blended. Heat a small (6- to 8-inch) skillet over medium heat until hot enough to sizzle a drop of water. Add the remaining 1 teaspoon oil and tilt the pan to coat evenly. Add the eggs and cook, covered, adjusting the heat as needed, until the eggs are set, 2 to 3 minutes. Use a rubber spatula to slide the omelet from the pan onto a plate. Cut the omelet in half and set aside.

3 Place the sliced onion in a small bowl and add cold water to cover. Swish the water around with your fingers or a fork. Drain the onions in a strainer and rinse well with cold water. Blot dry with a kitchen towel. Combine the onions and vinegar in a small bowl and set aside.

4 To assemble each *torta*, lay a roll on your work surface, cut side up. On the bottom half of each, place 1 or 2 rounded table-spoons of the pinto beans, pressing them into the bread with the back of a fork to make a ¼-inch-thick layer. (Serve the extra pinto beans on the side.) Top with thin slices of onion, dividing evenly. Top with the omelet, folding it to fit, if necessary. Add 1 or 2 tablespoons of Cactus Salad and top with the shredded lettuce, dividing evenly. (Serve the extra Cactus Salad on the side as well.) Mash the chunks of avocado into the other half of the roll, dividing evenly. If you like your *torta* spicy, shake a few drops of hot sauce, or more to taste, on top of the lettuce.

5 Press the top of the roll onto the sand-wich to compress the ingredients. Wrap in foil and set aside until ready to serve.

Green Pozole, page 108

SOUPS

Chilled Borscht with Cucumber and Apple

This is a version of a cold beet soup I enjoyed on a warm summer day while traveling in St. Petersburg, Russia. It was served icy cold, with a few bits of chopped apple and cucumber floating in the bowl. In my version, I add more apple and cucumber. These crunchy vegetables contrast perfectly with the soft texture of the beets. **MAKES 4 TO 6 SERVINGS**

1½ to 2 pounds beets (about 4 large), trimmed and scrubbed clean

1 cup chopped ripe tomato or drained diced canned tomatoes

2 garlic cloves

1 medium onion, cut into thick slices

1 large sprig fresh flat-leaf (Italian) parsley, including the stem

1 large sprig fresh dill, including the stem, plus more for garnish, plus ¼ cup chopped dill

1 leafy celery top

2 strips (about 2 x ½ inches) orange zest, folded to release the oils

6 whole black peppercorns

6 dried allspice berries

2 teaspoons coarse salt, or to taste

6 cups water

1 large crisp apple, peeled, cored, and coarsely chopped (about 2 cups)

1 cucumber, seeded if seeds are large, coarsely chopped (about 2 cups)

6 tablespoons apple cider vinegar, or more to taste

1 tablespoon honey

½ teaspoon coarsely ground black pepper

1 cup sour cream or plain whole-milk yogurt

1 Combine the beets, tomatoes, garlic, onion, parsley, dill sprig, celery, orange zest, peppercorns, allspice, and salt in a large soup pot. Add the water and bring to a boil. Reduce the heat to medium-low and simmer, covered, until the tip of a paring knife slips easily into the beets, about 25 minutes. Let cool slightly.

2 With a slotted spoon, lift the beets from the broth and set aside until cool enough to handle. Meanwhile, strain the broth into a large bowl and discard the solids. Refrigerate the broth to chill it.

3 Add the apples to the broth in the refrigerator. Do the same with the cucumber. When the beets are cool enough to handle, slip off their skins and the rough knob where the tops were attached. Cut the beets into ½-inch pieces and coarsely chop

them in a food processor. Remove the broth from the refrigerator and stir in the beets.

4 Add the vinegar, chopped dill, honey, and pepper to the broth and gently stir to combine. Cover and refrigerate until well chilled, at least 2 hours. To serve, ladle into bowls, top with a spoonful of sour cream, and garnish with a few small sprigs of dill.

Creamy Yogurt, Ground Walnut, and Cucumber Soup

This simple, refreshing summer soup comes from a dear friend, Nadia Merzliakov, who learned it from her cousins who live in Sofia, Bulgaria. The soup can be made in just a few minutes and, if all the ingredients are cold, will be ready to eat without waiting for it to be chilled. **MAKES 4 SERVINGS**

½ cup chopped walnuts

2 slender cucumbers, peeled and cut into ½-inch cubes (about 4 cups)

¼ cup chopped fresh dill

1 garlic clove, chopped

1 teaspoon coarse salt

1 quart (32 ounces) plain whole-milk Greek-style yogurt

2 tablespoons finely chopped fresh mint

1 Place two ice cubes in a 1-cup measure and add water to measure 1 cup. Let stand until the ice is melted and the water is "ice cold."

2 Finely chop the walnuts in a food processor; transfer to a large bowl. Finely chop the cucumbers, dill, and garlic together in the food processor. Transfer to the bowl with the walnuts. Stir in the salt. Add the yogurt and gently fold to combine. The soup will be very thick.

3 Add enough of the ice water, 1 tablespoon at a time, to the soup until it is the consistency of heavy cream. Ladle into bowls and serve with a pinch of the chopped mint on top.

Variation

To make a version with a kick, add 1 to 2 teaspoons finely chopped jalapeño or other hot chile.

Tortilla Soup

This silky-smooth version of tortilla soup is flavored by the sweetness of caramelized onion, a generous shot of tequila, the heat of a pureed ancho chile and fresh jalapeños, and a hit of cumin. Half of the tortillas are simmered in the broth, which imparts the rich taste of corn to the soup. The remaining tortillas are crisped and piled into the large soup bowls, along with avocado slices, crumbled cotija cheese, and snipped cilantro leaves before the hot soup is ladled in. Pass lime wedges at the table so everyone can add a squirt of lime juice. MAKES 4 TO 6 SERVINGS

2 tablespoons extra-virgin olive oil

1½ cups chopped onion

Pinch of sugar

2 garlic cloves, grated or finely chopped

½ cup tequila

2 dried ancho chiles (see page 88)

2 cups boiling water

2 teaspoons cumin seeds or 2 teaspoons ground cumin

1 can (28 ounces) plum tomatoes with their juices

3 to 4 cups Roasted Vegetable Broth (page 120)

3 (6-inch) corn tortillas, torn into 1-inch pieces, plus 6 tortillas, left whole

¼ cup chopped seeded jalapeño pepper

1 teaspoon coarse salt, plus more to taste

½ teaspoon dried oregano

¼ teaspoon freshly ground black pepper, plus more to taste

Vegetable oil, such as corn oil, as needed

1 large or 2 small avocados, peeled, pitted, and cut into thin wedges

½ cup coarsely chopped fresh cilantro (including stems)

1 cup crumbled or shredded cotija cheese (see page 249)

8 lime wedges

1 Heat the olive oil in a large heavy pot or Dutch oven over medium heat until hot enough to sizzle a piece of onion. Add the onion and sprinkle with the sugar. Reduce the heat to very low and cook the onion slowly, stirring often, until it is caramelized, about 45 minutes. Add the garlic and cook, stirring, for about 1 minute. Add the tequila, bring to a boil, lower the heat, and simmer until reduced by half, about 3 minutes.

2 While the onion is cooking, heat a heavy skillet over medium-high heat until hot. Add the ancho chiles and toast for about 3 minutes on each side, until they soften and puff up slightly. Transfer the chiles to a bowl and add the boiling water. Let stand until the chiles are softened, about 30 minutes. Set a strainer over a bowl and strain the liquid from the chiles. Reserve the liquid. Remove the stems and seeds from the chiles and discard. Tear the chiles into 2-inch pieces and add them to the onion.

3 Place the cumin seeds or ground cumin in a small dry skillet over low heat; slowly toast the seeds, shaking the pan, until the cumin is fragrant and one shade darker. If using cumin seeds, transfer to a spice grinder and grind. Add the cumin to the onions.

4 Add the tomatoes, reserved chile soaking liquid, 3 cups of the broth, the torn pieces of tortilla, jalapeños, salt, oregano, and pepper to the pot with the onions. Bring to a boil and simmer, covered, for about 30 minutes. Uncover and let cool until lukewarm.

5 Working in batches, puree the soup in a blender until smooth. Return to the pot. Alternatively, the soup can be pureed directly in the pot using an immersion blender. If the soup is too thick, add the remaining 1 cup broth. Add more salt and pepper to taste, if needed.

6 To make the fried tortilla strips, cut the reserved 6 whole tortillas into ¼- to ½-inch-wide strips. Heat about ½ inch of vegetable oil in a skillet until hot enough

to sizzle a piece of tortilla. Add half of the tortilla strips and fry, stirring carefully with a large fork, until crisp and a shade darker. Use a slotted spoon to remove to a layer of paper towels spread on a tray. Repeat with the remaining tortilla strips.

Alternatively, to make oven-baked tortilla strips, preheat the oven to 375°F. Lightly brush the whole tortillas on one side with vegetable oil. Stack the tortillas and cut them into strips. Spread on one or two baking sheets and bake until crisp, stirring once, 12 to 15 minutes.

7 When ready to serve the soup, place a handful of crisp tortilla strips, 3 or 4 avocado slices, 2 tablespoons of the cilantro, and about ¼ cup of the crumbled cheese in each bowl. Ladle the hot soup on top. Squeeze a wedge of lime into each bowl and serve with additional lime wedges on the side.

Ancho Chiles
Ancho is the dried form of the poblano chile. It is dark red, almost black, with crinkly skin and a mild to hot taste. It must be toasted in a hot, dry skillet and then soaked in hot water to reconstitute before using. Typically anchos are pureed into sauces or soups.

Golden Potato and Sofrito Soup with Parsley Alioli

In Spanish cooking, a finely chopped mixture of peppers, onions, and garlic slowly sautéed in olive oil with a bay leaf is called sofrito. In this case, the sofrito is combined with potatoes to make a thick, stewlike soup. Each portion is topped with a spoonful of alioli, a classic Spanish sauce heady with garlic and flecked green with parsley. The potatoes are split with two forks or pulled apart with the tip of a chef's knife, rather than cut into chunks, which contributes to the texture. I learned this unusual technique from the cookbook author Penelope Casas, and this recipe is inspired by one from her book *Delicioso, The Regional Cooking of Spain*. **MAKES 4 TO 6 SERVINGS**

Soup

- 3 tablespoons extra-virgin olive oil
- 1¾ cups finely chopped onion
- 1¾ cups finely chopped red bell pepper
- 2 garlic cloves, minced
- 1 bay leaf
- ½ teaspoon coarse salt
- 3 pounds all-purpose white potatoes, peeled
- 2 teaspoons pimentón de la Vera (see page 26) or other smoked paprika
- Freshly ground black pepper
- 4 cups Roasted Vegetable Broth (page 120)
- 1 small dried red chile (optional)

Parsley Alioli

- 2 large egg yolks
- 3 garlic cloves
- ½ teaspoon coarse salt
- 1 cup extra-virgin olive oil
- 1 teaspoon fresh lemon juice
- ½ teaspoon cold water
- 2 tablespoons finely chopped fresh flat-leaf (Italian) parsley

1 Make the soup: Heat the oil over medium-low heat in a large soup pot until hot enough to sizzle a piece of onion. Add the onion and bell pepper and cook, stirring, over low heat until the vegetables are softened and golden, about 20 minutes. Add the garlic, bay leaf, and salt and cook, stirring, for about 5 minutes.

2 To prepare the potatoes, break them into 1- to 1½-inch chunks by inserting the tip of a sturdy knife (a chef's knife works best) or two forks into the center of the potato and pulling the potato apart, creating jagged

surfaces. If this doesn't work for you, cut the potatoes into irregularly shaped pieces.

3 Add the pimentón to the onions and stir to combine. Add the potatoes and cook over medium-low heat, covered, stirring occasionally to prevent sticking, for about 20 minutes.

4 Add the broth and chile, if using, and bring to a boil. Reduce the heat to medium-low and cook, covered, until the potatoes are very soft and thicken the broth, about 25 minutes. Remove the bay leaf.

5 While the potatoes are cooking, make the Parsley Alioli: Combine the egg yolks, garlic, and salt in a food processor and pulse to blend. With the motor running, very slowly add about ⅓ cup of the oil, one drop at a time, until the mixture begins to thicken. Add the lemon juice and the water in a slow trickle, then add the remaining ⅔ cup oil in a slow, steady stream until the sauce has the consistency of mayonnaise. Add the parsley and pulse just to blend. Taste and add more salt, if needed.

6 To serve, ladle the soup into bowls and spoon a dollop of Parsley Alioli on top.

Lentil, Eggplant, and Barley Soup with Tahini

Soups and stews brimming with legumes, grains, and vegetables are prepared throughout the Middle East. This recipe, enriched with tahini (ground sesame seeds), is adapted from an Iraqi recipe for a lentil and chickpea stew. The tahini contributes a noticeably creamy mouthfeel with only an intriguing hint of its distinctive taste. MAKES 4 TO 6 SERVINGS

2 medium eggplants (each about 10 to 12 ounces)

2 tablespoons extra-virgin olive oil

2 cups chopped onion

2 garlic cloves, chopped

¼ teaspoon crushed red pepper flakes

1 teaspoon ground turmeric

1 teaspoon ground cumin

6 to 8 cups Roasted Vegetable Broth (page 120)

¼ cup pearl barley

1 cup canned diced or whole tomatoes, cut up, with their juices

1 cup diced (½-inch pieces) peeled carrot

⅓ cup brown lentils

1 teaspoon coarse salt, or more to taste

⅛ teaspoon freshly ground black pepper, or more to taste

¼ cup tahini (see page 41), or more to taste

2 cups loosely packed torn and stemmed leaf spinach or baby spinach

2 tablespoons fresh lemon juice

¼ cup *each* chopped cilantro, dill, and/or mint, for garnish (optional)

1 Preheat the oven to 400°F and line a baking sheet with foil. Prick the skins on the eggplants about 6 times with the tip of a paring knife. Place the eggplants on the foil and roast until soft and shriveled, 30 to 45 minutes, depending on their size. Wrap in the foil and let cool.

2 While the eggplants are roasting, heat the oil in a large, broad soup pot or Dutch oven until hot enough to sizzle a piece of onion. Add the onion, garlic, and red pepper flakes and cook, stirring, over medium heat until the onion is golden, about 6 minutes. Stir in the turmeric and cumin.

3 Add 6 cups of the broth and the barley to the sautéed onion mixture and bring to a boil. Cover and cook over medium-low heat for about 45 minutes. The barley will not be fully cooked.

4 When the eggplants are cool enough to handle, peel off the skins with a paring knife and discard. Quarter the eggplants and scoop out any seeds in the center with the tip of a teaspoon. Discard the seeds. Chop the eggplant flesh; you should have about 1½ cups.

5 Add the eggplant, tomatoes, carrots, lentils, salt, and black pepper to the pot and bring the soup to a boil. Cover and cook over medium-low heat until the lentils, carrots, and barley are all tender, about 25 minutes. Stir in the tahini. Add more broth to thin the soup to the desired consistency, if needed.

6 Taste the soup and add more salt, pepper, or tahini, if needed. Stir in the spinach and cook until wilted, about 2 minutes. Add the lemon juice. Ladle into bowls and sprinkle the top generously with the cilantro, dill, and/or mint, if using.

Curried Coconut Milk and Tofu Soup with Bok Choy

To flavor this hearty, soul-warming Thai-style curried coconut soup, reach for your trusty tin of Madras curry. That and a few Thai essentials—galangal, ginger, lemongrass, garlic, shallots, and chiles—and you're ready to go. The whole soup is ready to serve in less than 30 minutes. **MAKES 4 SMALL SERVINGS OR 2 LARGE SERVINGS**

¼ cup sliced (½-inch pieces) lemongrass

2 tablespoons chopped peeled fresh ginger

2 tablespoons chopped galangal (optional; see box)

2 garlic cloves, bruised with the side of a knife

¼ cup coarsely chopped shallot

1 serrano chile, thinly sliced, or more to taste

2 curry leaves, slivered (see page 34); optional

1 tablespoon Madras curry powder (see page 279), or more to taste

2 cans (13.5 ounces each) coconut milk

2 cups water

¼ cup coarsely chopped fresh cilantro stems

8 ounces silken tofu, cut into large irregular-shaped pieces

4 small heads baby bok choy, trimmed and thinly sliced (about 2 cups), covered with cold water in a bowl to crisp

¼ cup finely chopped fresh cilantro or Thai basil

1 Pound the lemongrass, ginger, galangal (if using), garlic, shallots, chile, and curry leaves (if using) in a large heavy mortar with a pestle or finely chop; set aside.

2 Sprinkle the curry powder in a large deep saucepan and heat, stirring, over low heat until fragrant. Add the lemongrass mixture, coconut milk, water, and cilantro stems. Heat, stirring, just until the mixture is steaming. Remove from the heat, cover, and let stand for 20 minutes to steep.

3 Strain the soup into a bowl, pressing down on the solids to extract the flavors. Discard the solids and return the strained soup to the saucepan. Taste and add more chiles or other seasonings, if desired.

4 Add the tofu. Drain the bok choy and add it to the soup. Warm over medium heat until hot, about 10 minutes. Ladle into bowls and sprinkle with the cilantro.

Galangal

Galangal is in the same family as ginger but is more aromatic. It can be hard to find fresh and is often in the freezer in Asian markets. Dried galangal is not a suitable substitute. Omit the fresh galangal, if none is available.

Creamy Peanut and Sweet Potato Soup

Chefs have a tendency to embellish this soup—popular in Africa—with coconut milk, crushed pineapple, and sometimes chicken. I've kept this version simple. Made with pureed sweet potatoes and peanut butter thinned with vegetable broth, it is a rich, smooth soup made lively with a garnish of chopped roasted peanuts, jalapeño, and cilantro, and brightened with a squirt of lime juice. **MAKES 4 TO 6 SERVINGS**

1 tablespoon extra-virgin olive oil

1 cup chopped onion

1 tablespoon chopped peeled fresh ginger

1 tablespoon chopped garlic

1 tablespoon ground cumin

1 tablespoon ground coriander

¼ teaspoon ground red pepper or cayenne pepper, or to taste

5 cups Roasted Vegetable Broth (page 120)

1 can (15 ounces) diced tomatoes with their juices

1¾ pounds moist orange-fleshed sweet potatoes (sometimes called yams), peeled and cut into ½-inch chunks (about 6 cups)

1 teaspoon coarse salt

½ teaspoon freshly ground black pepper

½ cup creamy peanut butter

2 tablespoons fresh lime juice

½ cup finely chopped roasted lightly salted peanuts

½ cup finely chopped fresh cilantro

1 jalapeño pepper, seeded and finely chopped

1 Heat the oil in a large saucepan or soup pot over medium heat until hot enough to sizzle a piece of onion. Add the onion, ginger, and garlic and cook, stirring, over medium-low heat until softened and golden, about 10 minutes. Add the cumin, coriander, and red pepper and heat, stirring, for about 30 seconds.

2 Add the broth, tomatoes, sweet potatoes, salt, and black pepper and bring to a boil. Reduce the heat to low, and cook, covered, until the sweet potatoes are tender, about 15 to 20 minutes depending on the variety of sweet potato. Stir in the peanut butter until blended. Remove from the heat and let the soup cool slightly.

3 Puree the soup, in batches, in a blender until it is thick and smooth. Return to the pot and reheat until steaming. Taste and add more salt and pepper, if needed. Stir in the lime juice.

4 Ladle into large bowls and garnish each serving with the peanuts, cilantro, and jalapeño.

Pureed Beet and Egg Soup

Until I happened upon a pureed beet and egg soup recipe in a collection of Old World recipes attributed to Eastern European or Russian kitchens, I thought I'd tasted every kind of beet soup in the world. When beaten into the steaming hot soup, the eggs turn this soup into something gloriously creamy and sophisticated. **MAKES 4 SERVINGS**

4 cups water

1 pound beets (save the tops, if attached, for another use), scrubbed, trimmed, peeled, and coarsely chopped (3 to 4 cups)

1 small parsnip, trimmed, peeled, and coarsely chopped (about 1 cup)

1 medium onion, coarsely chopped (about 1 cup)

4 tablespoons apple cider vinegar, plus more to taste

1 bay leaf

1 teaspoon coarse salt, plus more to taste

¼ teaspoon coarsely ground black pepper, plus more to taste

4 large eggs

¼ cup finely chopped fresh dill, plus 4 dill sprigs for garnish

1 cup sour cream

1 Combine the water, beets, parsnip, onion, vinegar, bay leaf, salt, and pepper in a medium saucepan and bring to a boil. Reduce the heat to medium-low, cover, and simmer until the vegetables are very tender, about 25 minutes. Cool slightly. Remove the bay leaf.

2 Working in batches, if necessary, puree the beets and liquid in a blender until very smooth. Transfer back to the saucepan and bring to a gentle boil. Meanwhile, whisk the eggs in a heatproof bowl until light. Slowly pour about half of the hot soup into the eggs, whisking gently to combine. Return to the saucepan with the rest of the soup and warm over very low heat. *Do not let the soup boil or the eggs will curdle.* Taste and add more vinegar, 1 tablespoon at a time, if needed, and additional salt and pepper, if desired. Stir in the chopped dill.

3 Ladle the soup into bowls and top each with a spoonful of sour cream and garnish with the dill sprigs.

Cold Saffron and Yogurt Soup

There are many variations of cold yogurt-based soups served throughout the Middle East, but I am especially fond of this pretty golden-hued Persian soup with the distinctive taste of saffron. Ground walnuts thicken it as it stands. When pomegranates are in season, sprinkle a few of the juicy red seeds onto the surface of each bowl of soup. If pomegranates are not available, the thin drizzle of pomegranate molasses will suffice.

MAKES 3 OR 4 SERVINGS

¼ teaspoon crumbled saffron threads

½ cup boiling water

3 cups plain whole-milk or low-fat yogurt

2 cups peeled and cubed (½-inch pieces) cucumbers, plus 1 cup finely diced cucumber

¾ cup coarsely chopped sweet white onion

2 tablespoons coarsely chopped fresh mint leaves

2 tablespoons coarsely chopped fresh dill, including stems, plus ¼ cup dill leaves for garnish

1 teaspoon coarse salt, plus more to taste

½ cup broken walnuts

2 tablespoons pomegranate molasses (see page 26)

2 tablespoons pomegranate seeds, for garnish (optional)

1 Place the saffron in a small bowl and add the boiling water. Cover and let stand for about 15 minutes.

2 Puree the yogurt, the 2 cups cubed cucumber, and ½ cup of the onion in a food processor or blender until smooth. Transfer to a large bowl. Stir in the saffron water, making sure to include all the pieces of saffron, the 1 cup finely diced cucumber, 1 tablespoon of the mint, 1 tablespoon of the chopped dill, and the salt until well blended.

3 Place the walnuts, the remaining ¼ cup onion, the remaining 1 tablespoon each of mint and chopped dill, and 1 tablespoon of the pomegranate molasses in the food processor and process until the mixture is pureed to a paste. Stir into the soup until well blended.

4 Cover the soup and chill until very cold, 3 to 4 hours. If the soup is too thick, add 1 to 2 tablespoons of cold water, or more as needed, to thin. To serve, ladle into bowls, drizzle each with a little of the remaining 1 tablespoon pomegranate molasses, and sprinkle with the pomegranate seeds, if using. Garnish each serving generously with the dill leaves.

Carrot and Yogurt Soup

This silken soup, the color of the setting sun, is tinged with the flavor of mustard seeds and the sweetness of fresh carrots. In India, black mustard seeds are popular, but in a pinch, yellow mustard seeds can be substituted. This soup uses the Indian technique of heating the mustard seeds in oil (or ghee) until they pop. Serve the soup either chilled or hot, but when reheating, do not let the soup boil or the yogurt might curdle. Ghee, the fat of choice in Indian cooking, is clarified butter and is easily made in about 15 minutes (see page 76). If you don't have any on hand, use vegetable oil.

MAKES 4 TO 6 SERVINGS

1 tablespoon ghee (see page 76) or vegetable oil

1 tablespoon brown or black mustard seeds (see page 100)

1 pound carrots, peeled, trimmed, and cut into ½-inch chunks

1 large onion, cut into ½-inch chunks

1 tablespoon chopped peeled fresh ginger

1 serrano chile, seeded and coarsely chopped (optional)

1 garlic clove, chopped

2 teaspoons Madras curry powder (see page 279)

4 cups water

¼ cup coarsely chopped cilantro, including tender stems, plus 2 tablespoons finely chopped leaves for garnish

2 teaspoons coarse salt

2 cups plain whole-milk or low-fat yogurt

1 Heat the ghee in a large heavy saucepan or soup pot over medium-high heat. Add the mustard seeds and cook, watching carefully, until the seeds begin to pop, about 1 minute. Add the carrots, onion, ginger, serrano chile (if using), and garlic and cook over medium heat, stirring, until the onion begins to wilt but does not brown, about 10 minutes. Add the curry powder and cook, stirring, for about 1 minute.

2 Add the water, the coarsely chopped cilantro, and the salt and bring to a boil. Cover and cook over medium heat until the carrots are tender, 20 to 25 minutes. Remove from the heat, uncover, and let stand until slightly cooled. Puree in a food processor or blender, working in batches, until very smooth.

3 Transfer the carrot puree to a large bowl and gradually stir in the yogurt until blended. If serving the soup cold, refrigerate for at least 4 hours or overnight. If serving the soup hot, transfer to a large saucepan and heat it, stirring, over medium-low heat. Do not let the soup boil or the yogurt might curdle. Ladle into bowls and garnish each with a shower of cilantro leaves.

Black Mustard Seeds

Mustard has been grown in India for thousands of years. Related to the Brassica family (as in cabbage, broccoli, etc.), it comes in at least three colors: black-brown, red-brown, and white or yellow. In Indian cooking, the darker-colored seeds are heated in oil until they pop, which toasts the seeds, flavors the oil, and intensifies the sweet mellow taste of the mustard. If they are not available, you can use the more common yellow mustard seeds.

White Bean Soup with Vegetables

A classic in Greek cooking, this simple soup is known as *fassolatha*. Use large white lima beans, known as gigandes, or cannellini beans. (The large white lima beans from Idaho heirloom bean grower Zürzun are excellent.) It is a simple soup using whatever basics are on hand—celery, carrots, onions—and is seasoned with parsley, mint, and/or oregano. If you choose to use dried mint and oregano instead of fresh, finely chop the dried herbs along with the fresh parsley to get a jump-start on rehydrating them. The addition of fresh lemon juice just before serving heightens the flavors and is essential. MAKES 6 SERVINGS

12 ounces (about 2 cups) large lima or cannellini beans

2 tablespoons extra-virgin olive oil

2 cups chopped onion or leeks (white and pale green parts)

1 cup chopped celery, including leaves

1 cup chopped peeled carrot

8 cups water

1 bay leaf

2 tablespoons tomato paste

1 teaspoon coarse salt, plus more to taste

Freshly ground black pepper

2 tablespoons finely chopped fresh flat-leaf (Italian) parsley

2 tablespoons finely chopped fresh mint or 1 teaspoon dried mint

1 tablespoon finely chopped fresh oregano leaves or 1 teaspoon dried oregano

¼ cup fresh lemon juice

1 Place the beans in a large bowl and cover with cold water. Let stand for 6 hours or overnight. Drain.

2 Heat the oil in a large soup pot over medium-low heat, add the onion, and cook until golden, about 10 minutes. Add the celery and carrots and cook, stirring occasionally, for about 5 minutes more.

3 Add the beans, the water, and the bay leaf and bring to a boil. Reduce the heat and simmer, partially covered, for about 1 hour. Stir in the tomato paste, salt, and a grinding of black pepper. If using the dried herbs chopped with the parsley, add them now. Simmer until the beans are soft and creamy, another 30 minutes to 1 hour. If using all fresh herbs, add them here. Add salt, to taste. Remove the bay leaf.

4 Just before serving, add the lemon juice.

Roasted Tomato and Cannellini Bean Soup

If you have Roasted Vegetable Broth and Roasted Plum Tomatoes on hand, this satisfying pureed soup comes together in less than 20 minutes. I make the roasted tomatoes in the summer when the tomato harvest is best and freeze them to use in soups and sauces throughout the year. You can use boxed vegetable broth and canned fire-roasted tomatoes in a pinch, but not with the same stellar results. MAKES 4 SERVINGS

1 tablespoon extra-virgin olive oil

1 cup finely chopped onion

2 cups cooked dried cannellini beans, or 1 can (15 ounces), drained and rinsed

2 tablespoons finely chopped fresh flat-leaf (Italian) parsley

2 cups Roasted Plum Tomatoes with their juices (recipe follows) or canned fire-roasted tomatoes with their juices

4 cups Roasted Vegetable Broth (page 120)

¼ cup grated Parmigiano-Reggiano, plus more if desired

Coarse salt and freshly ground black pepper

1 Heat the oil in a large heavy saucepan until hot enough to sizzle a piece of onion. Add the onion, reduce the heat to low, and cook, stirring, until the onion begins to turn golden but is not browned, 8 to 10 minutes. Add the beans and the parsley and stir to combine.

2 Puree the tomatoes in a food processor. Add the puree to the beans, stir in the broth, and bring to a boil. Reduce the heat and simmer for about 10 minutes. Stir in the cheese. Taste and add salt and pepper, if needed.

3 Ladle into bowls and, if desired, top each with a shower of additional cheese.

Roasted Plum Tomatoes

One pound of ripe plum tomatoes (about 6 large) will yield 1 cup of roasted tomatoes. I usually roast 3 pounds—just enough to fill a large baking sheet comfortably—at a time and freeze in 1- or 2-cup portions to use later. They are delicious pureed or coarsely chopped. Use for a quick tomato sauce for pasta, as a base for soup (page 102), stirred into risotto, or on top of baked potatoes. MAKES ABOUT 3 CUPS

3 pounds ripe plum tomatoes (about 18 large), stems removed, halved lengthwise

2 tablespoons extra-virgin olive oil

2 garlic cloves, thinly sliced

2 sprigs basil, left whole

½ teaspoon coarse salt

⅛ teaspoon coarsely ground black pepper

1 Preheat the oven to 400°F.

2 Spread the tomatoes on a large baking sheet. Arrange some of the tomatoes cut side up and some cut side down. Drizzle with the oil. Place the garlic and basil randomly on top of the tomatoes. Sprinkle evenly with the salt and pepper.

3 Roast until the skins of the tomatoes are blistered and the tomatoes look shriveled, 35 to 45 minutes. Let cool. Discard the basil. Place the tomatoes in containers and refrigerate or freeze until ready to use. They will keep in the refrigerator for 4 or 5 days or in the freezer for 3 months or more.

Kabocha Squash, Coriander, and Coconut Soup with Peanuts

I am drawn to the thick, pasty texture and intense sweet taste of kabocha squash. This soup, made with steamed kabocha, is a silken puree of coconut milk heady with lightly toasted ground coriander. MAKES 4 SERVINGS

2½ pounds kabocha, or other firm-fleshed dark orange squash, cut into large chunks, seeds and membranes discarded

2 tablespoons vegetable oil

1 cup diced (½-inch pieces) onion

1 garlic clove, smashed with the side of a knife

1 teaspoon grated peeled fresh ginger

2 teaspoons ground coriander

2 cans (13.5 ounces each) coconut milk

1 tablespoon tomato paste

1 dried red chile

Coarse salt

2 tablespoons fresh lime juice

1 cup Roasted Vegetable Broth (page 120), water, or apple juice, as needed

¼ cup finely chopped fresh cilantro, including the thin stems

¼ cup finely chopped lightly salted dry-roasted peanuts

1 Place the squash in a steamer basket and place over 1 inch of boiling water. Steam, covered, until the squash is very tender when pierced with the tip of a knife, about 20 minutes. Remove from the heat and let cool. When cool enough to handle, scoop the tender squash from the hard skin with a tablespoon. Discard the skin.

2 Meanwhile, heat the oil in a large, wide saucepan until hot enough to sizzle a piece of onion. Add the onion and cook, stirring, over medium-low heat, until the onion is translucent and beginning to turn golden, about 10 minutes. Add the garlic, ginger, and coriander and cook over low heat, stirring, for about 1 minute.

3 Stir in the coconut milk and tomato paste. Puree the mixture, in batches, in a food processor or blender until very smooth. Return to the saucepan. Add the chile and bring to a gentle boil. Cover and cook over low heat for about 10 minutes. Add salt to taste.

4 Stir in the lime juice. If the soup is too thick, thin to the desired consistency with the broth. Ladle into bowls and sprinkle the top with the cilantro and peanuts.

Shiitake Mushroom and Ginger Congee

The original inspiration for this classic Chinese soup is a thick rice porridge served as a breakfast dish. I love this vegetarian version—dark and flavorful from dried shiitake mushrooms and heady with the heat and aroma of peeled fresh ginger—any time of the day. **MAKES 4 SERVINGS**

6 cups Shiitake Mushroom Broth (page 119)

Coarse salt (optional)

Soy sauce (optional)

¾ cup short-grain brown or white rice, rinsed and drained

1 cup (about 3 ounces) snow peas, stems trimmed, stringed, and cut on the diagonal into ¼-inch slices

½ cup julienned (⅛-x-1-inch pieces) scallion (green parts only)

2 tablespoons julienned (⅛-x-1-inch pieces) peeled fresh ginger

¼ cup chopped dry-roasted unsalted peanuts

Sesame chile oil (optional; see page 60)

1 Taste the broth and add more salt or soy sauce, if needed. Add the rice and bring to a boil. Cook, covered, until the rice is very soft and the soup is thickened, about 55 minutes for brown rice or 25 minutes for white rice.

2 Bring a small saucepan half filled with water to a boil. Add the snow peas and cook for about 30 seconds. Drain, rinse with cold water to cool, and pat dry with a paper towel. In a small bowl, combine the snow peas, scallions, and ginger.

3 When the rice is cooked, spoon the rice and broth into bowls. The mixture will be very thick. Add hot water to thin, if desired. Top each bowl with some of the scallion mixture. Sprinkle each with the peanuts, dividing evenly. Serve with sesame chile oil drizzled on top, to taste, if desired.

Green Pozole

The word *pozole* refers to both a stewlike soup and the kernels of hominy that it contains. Hominy is made by soaking dried corn in slaked lime to remove the hull and then boiling it until tender. Fortunately, it is widely available canned. Pozole (the soup) comes in many forms, some with the addition of seafood, poultry, beef, and/or pork, and some without. This variation is made entirely with vegetables. The soup is thickened with masa harina; in this case, fine-ground cornmeal can be substituted. The platter of garnishes—avocado, radishes, red onion slices, cilantro, crumbled cheese, toasted salted pepitas, lime wedges, and chopped serrano or jalapeño peppers—help make it a hearty meal. **MAKES 4 TO 6 SERVINGS**

Pozole

- 1 poblano chile
- 6 cups water
- 6 sprigs fresh cilantro, including tender stems
- 4 serrano chiles, stems removed, halved lengthwise, and seeded (or leave the seeds for added heat)
- 4 garlic cloves, smashed with the side of a knife
- 2 large (6 to 8 ounces each) white potatoes, peeled and cut into quarters
- 1 can (14 ounces) hominy, rinsed and drained
- 1 pound tomatillos (see page 110), husked, rinsed, trimmed, and cut into ½-inch pieces
- 1 large white onion, cut into ½-inch pieces
- 1 large carrot, peeled, halved lengthwise, and cut into ¼-inch pieces
- 1 celery stalk, including leaves, cut into ¼-inch slices
- 2 teaspoons coarse salt, plus more to taste
- 1 teaspoon dried epazote (see page 110) or Mexican oregano (see page 110)

- 1 tablespoon vegetable oil
- 8 ounces mushrooms (any type), trimmed and cut into ½-inch pieces
- 3 cups lightly packed coarsely chopped Swiss chard, collards, or kale (tough stems removed)
- 1 ear corn, trimmed and cut into 1-inch-thick rounds, or 1 cup fresh, canned, or frozen corn kernels
- 2 tablespoons masa harina (see page 70) or fine cornmeal
- ¼ cup fresh lime juice

Garnishes

- 1 or 2 avocados, peeled, pitted, and cut into ¼-inch wedges
- ½ cup thinly sliced radish
- ½ cup Salted Toasted Pepitas (recipe follows)
- ½ cup finely chopped fresh cilantro
- ½ cup crumbled queso fresco, shredded cotija, or other cheese (see page 249)
- ½ cup chopped red onion
- 2 limes, cut into wedges

1 Make the pozole: Position the broiler shelf so that it's about 3 inches from the heat source. Line a baking sheet with foil and place the poblano on the foil. Broil, turning the poblano as it blisters and chars, until evenly blackened, about 5 minutes per side. Remove from the broiler and wrap in the foil. Once cool, unwrap and rub off the charred skin. Remove and discard the stems and seeds. Coarsely chop the poblano and place in a large soup pot.

2 To the soup pot, add the water, cilantro, serrano chiles, garlic, potatoes, hominy, tomatillos, onion, carrot, celery, salt, and epazote. Bring to a boil. Reduce the heat and simmer, covered, until the tomatillos are dissolved and the potatoes are tender, 20 to 25 minutes.

3 Heat the oil in a medium skillet and sauté the mushrooms, stirring, until lightly browned, about 5 minutes. Add to the soup pot. Stir in the chard and corn. Simmer, uncovered, for about 5 minutes. Taste and add more salt, if needed.

4 Add the masa harina to the soup, cover, and simmer, stirring occasionally, until the soup is slightly thickened, about 5 minutes. Just before serving, stir in the lime juice.

5 Serve the pozole: Set out a tray with the garnishes in separate serving dishes or displayed on a large platter. Ladle the pozole into large deep bowls. Top with the preferred garnishes and squeeze the juice from the lime wedges into the soup, as desired.

Salted Toasted Pepitas

Spread about 1/2 cup of pepitas (hulled pumpkin seeds) in a small skillet. Drizzle with 1 teaspoon vegetable oil and sprinkle lightly with salt. Cook, stirring constantly, over medium heat until the pepitas begin to turn golden brown and "pop" in the pan, about 2 minutes. Let cool.

Tomatillos

Tomatillos are also called Mexican green tomatoes. They are relatively small and have a thin papery covering that is easily peeled away. Their tartness can be tamed by first simmering them in water. They are gently boiled in water until almost dissolved before using in salsa, soups, and sauces.

Epazote

Epazote is a distinctively pungent, aromatic herb sold both dried and fresh in Mexican markets. Because of its strong flavor, it is used sparingly in stews, beans, and other cooked dishes. It also is reputed to make beans more digestible.

Mexican Oregano

A pungent herb related more to lemon verbena than to its Mediterranean namesake, Mexican oregano has a distinctive taste but if overused will make a dish bitter, so use it sparingly.

Red Lentil and Tomato Soup with Tamarind

Egyptian split red lentils, which cook quickly, are my choice for this tangy soup. Tamarind concentrate, available in jars in many groceries, adds tartness, which I balance with a drizzle of honey. A spoonful of yogurt and a shower of cilantro pull all the flavors together. **MAKES 6 SERVINGS**

8 cups water

1½ cups Egyptian red lentils

6 sprigs fresh cilantro, with stems, plus
¼ cup finely chopped fresh cilantro

2 teaspoons coarse salt, plus more to taste

2 cups diced (½-inch pieces) onion

1 tablespoon coarsely chopped peeled fresh ginger

2 tablespoons coarsely chopped garlic

1 or 2 serrano, jalapeño, or other fresh chile peppers, depending on desired heat (include seeds for more heat)

2 tablespoons vegetable oil

1 teaspoon whole cumin seeds

1 can (14.5 ounces) diced tomatoes with their juices

1 tablespoon tamarind paste

1 teaspoon ground turmeric

1 tablespoon honey, plus more to taste (optional)

1 cup plain whole-milk yogurt, whisked

1 Combine the water, lentils, and cilantro sprigs in a large saucepan and bring to a boil. Cover and cook over low heat until the lentils are very soft, anywhere from 10 to 30 minutes. Stir in the salt.

2 Meanwhile, finely chop the onion, ginger, garlic, and chiles in a food processor.

3 Heat the oil in a medium skillet until hot enough to sizzle a cumin seed. Add the cumin seeds and toast, stirring, for about 10 seconds. Add the onion mixture and cook, stirring, over medium heat until the moisture is evaporated and the onions begin to brown, about 5 minutes. Stir in the tomatoes, tamarind, and turmeric and bring to a boil. Cook, stirring, over medium heat until the mixture is very thick, about 5 minutes.

4 Add the tomato mixture to the lentils and bring to a boil. Reduce the heat and simmer, uncovered, stirring, until the soup is thickened, 10 to 15 minutes. Taste and if the soup is too tart, stir in the honey. Adjust the seasoning with additional salt or honey, if needed.

5 To serve, ladle the soup into bowls and top each with a dollop of yogurt and a sprinkling of the chopped cilantro.

Miso Soup with Shiitake Mushrooms, Bok Choy, and Soba Noodles

Miso—fermented soybean paste—is sold in the refrigerated section of many grocers, right next to the tofu. Available in a range of colors and flavor strengths, it is the basis of many Japanese dishes. I prefer white or yellow miso for this light, refreshing soup, which is made hearty with soba noodles, a tiny dice of pumpkin or winter squash, and finely sliced bok choy. Soba is a thin Japanese noodle made from buckwheat (a gluten-free cereal). But sometimes wheat flour has been added to the dough to keep the noodles from crumbling when cooked, so if you are gluten-intolerant, you will want to read the label carefully. Dried soba are available in some supermarkets and all Asian grocers. **MAKES 4 TO 6 SERVINGS**

8 medium or 6 large dried shiitake mushrooms

8 cups water

3 ounces soba (buckwheat) noodles

1 cup diced (¼-inch pieces) peeled and seeded pumpkin or winter squash, such as kabocha or butternut

⅔ cup white or yellow miso paste

2 or 3 small baby bok choy (about 3 ounces), thinly sliced (about 1 cup)

2 scallions (white and green parts), cut on the diagonal

1 Combine the mushrooms and water in a large saucepan and bring to a boil. Reduce the heat to low and simmer, covered, for about 30 minutes.

2 Meanwhile, bring a saucepan half filled with water to a boil. Add the soba noodles and cook, stirring often, until tender, about 4 minutes. Drain and transfer the noodles to a bowl. Cover with cold water and set aside.

3 With a slotted spoon, remove the mushrooms from the broth and transfer to a bowl to cool. Reserve the broth in the saucepan. When cool enough to handle, remove and discard the woody mushroom stems. Slice the mushroom caps into thin pieces. Return to the broth and add the squash. Add the miso and stir until blended. Bring the broth to a boil, reduce the heat, and simmer until the squash is tender, about 8 minutes. Stir in the bok choy and simmer, stirring, for about 2 minutes more.

4 Drain the soba and add to the soup. Reheat, then ladle into bowls and garnish with the scallions.

Hot and Sour Mushroom Soup

Most hot and sour soups contain small amounts of meat, but this version, made with a richly flavored shiitake mushroom broth, is an excellent vegetarian version. For a juxtaposition of soft and crunchy, cook the bok choy minimally so it balances the softness of the mushroom caps.

MAKES 2 TO 4 SERVINGS

6 cups Shiitake Mushroom Broth (page 119)

6 reserved soaked and softened dried shiitake mushrooms (from the broth), stems discarded, caps cut into thin slivers (about ½ cup)

½ teaspoon freshly ground black pepper, plus more to taste

1 small dried hot red chile pepper (optional)

3 tablespoons cornstarch

3 tablespoons water

2 tablespoons soy sauce, plus more to taste

2 tablespoons Chinese black vinegar (see box) or balsamic vinegar, plus more to taste

1 tablespoon toasted sesame oil (see page 221)

2 small heads baby bok choy, halved lengthwise, core removed, and cut crosswise into thin slices (about 2 cups)

1 cup fresh oyster mushrooms, including stems, cut into ½-inch pieces

5 ounces medium or firm tofu, patted dry and cut into ½-inch cubes (about 1 heaping cup)

½ cup thinly sliced scallion (white and green parts)

½ cup chopped water chestnuts, rinsed and blotted dry

1 large egg

Chile oil (see page 60)

1 In a large saucepan, combine the broth, shiitake mushroom caps, black pepper, and red chile, if using, and bring to a boil. Reduce the heat to low and cook, covered, for about 5 minutes.

2 In a small bowl, stir together the cornstarch and 2 tablespoons of the water until smooth. Stir the cornstarch mixture, soy sauce, vinegar, and sesame oil into the broth. Cook, stirring gently, until the soup thickens and boils. Reduce the heat to low to maintain a steady simmer.

3 Add the bok choy, oyster mushrooms, tofu, scallions, and water chestnuts and stir until blended.

Chinese Black Vinegar

The label will say *Chenkong* rice vinegar. It is black with a distinctive rich, mellow flavor. It is popular in cooking and as a dip. Aged balsamic vinegar works as a substitute.

4 In a small bowl, beat the egg and the remaining 1 tablespoon water until well blended. Slowly drizzle the egg in a thin stream over the surface of the hot simmering soup. As the egg sets, stir it gently with a chopstick or long fork to break it into thin strips. Taste and adjust the seasoning by adding more soy sauce, vinegar, and black pepper, if desired. Serve additional soy sauce, vinegar, black pepper, and chile oil at the table so each person can season the soup as desired.

Vegetable and Tomato Broth with Cheese and Egg Balls

Light and cheesy, these "egg balls" are quickly fried in a shallow pan of oil and then added to a vegetable broth that has been enhanced with pureed tomatoes. Rich and hearty, this soup is suitable as a main course with a simple salad and slices of toasted Italian bread drizzled with olive oil on the side. **MAKES 4 SERVINGS**

Cheese and Egg Balls

- 1¼ cups fine dry bread crumbs, or more as needed
- ⅔ cup grated Parmigiano-Reggiano
- ⅓ cup grated Pecorino Romano
- 2 tablespoons finely chopped fresh flat-leaf (Italian) parsley
- ½ teaspoon grated garlic
- ½ teaspoon coarse salt
- Freshly ground black pepper
- 5 large eggs
- Vegetable oil, for frying

Vegetable and Tomato Broth

- 3 cups Roasted Vegetable Broth (page 120)
- 1 can (28 ounces) plum tomatoes with their juices
- 2 or 3 fresh basil leaves
- Coarse salt
- Freshly ground black pepper

1 Make the Cheese and Egg Balls: Combine the bread crumbs, cheeses, parsley, garlic, salt, and a grinding of pepper in a large bowl. Whisk the eggs in a medium bowl, then add to the bread crumb mixture. Stir gently to combine. If the mixture is too moist, add more bread crumbs, 1 tablespoon at a time. The mixture will stiffen as it stands. If it is too soft to form into balls, refrigerate, covered, for about 20 minutes.

2 With dampened hands, shape the mixture into balls about 1 inch in diameter. You should have about 18. Place on a plate, cover, and refrigerate for 20 minutes to set.

3 Heat about ½ inch of oil in a large skillet over medium heat until shimmering or hot enough to lightly brown a crust of bread. Add the balls, a few at a time, and fry in two batches until golden, turning often, about 5 minutes. Use a slotted spoon to transfer to a paper towel–lined plate. Transfer to a baking sheet and keep warm in the oven set at the lowest temperature.

4 Make the broth: Place the broth in a large saucepan. Set a food mill over the saucepan and puree the tomatoes and their

juices into the broth. Or, if preferred, puree the tomatoes in a food processor and then add them to the broth. (Do not use canned tomato puree in this recipe, as it is too concentrated.) Add the basil. Bring the broth to a boil, then reduce the heat to low. Add the warm cheese and egg balls to the broth and gently simmer for about 15 minutes. Taste and season with salt and pepper, if needed.

5 To serve, ladle the soup into 4 bowls and distribute the cheese and egg balls evenly among them.

Shiitake Mushroom Broth

I like this mushroom broth when I need a pure, clean mushroom taste with a hint of Asian flavors such as ginger and scallion. This is an excellent broth for soups and stews. It also makes a deliciously simple soup with the addition of slivered scallions, chopped bok choy, tofu, and/or a few tablespoons of cooked rice or a handful of noodles. **MAKES ABOUT 6 CUPS**

8 cups water

1 cup chopped (1-inch pieces, cut on the diagonal) scallion (white and green parts)

1 cup chopped (1-inch pieces, cut on the diagonal) celery

½ cup coarsely chopped fresh ginger

4 garlic cloves, smashed with the side of a knife

1 ounce whole dried shiitake mushrooms (about 6 medium)

2 tablespoons soy sauce, plus more as needed

1 teaspoon coarse salt

1 Combine the water, scallions, celery, ginger, garlic, mushrooms, soy sauce, and salt in a large saucepan. Bring to a boil. Reduce the heat to medium-low and simmer, partially covered, for about 45 minutes.

2 Strain the broth into a large bowl. Retrieve the mushrooms from the strainer. Cut off the stems. Cut the caps into ⅛-inch slices and return to the broth. Discard the remaining solids. You should have about 6 cups of broth.

3 Use at once or transfer to freezer containers and freeze for 3 months or longer.

Roasted Vegetable Broth

A flavorful vegetable broth filled with the complex flavors of a variety of roasted vegetables is an excellent all-purpose homemade vegetable broth to keep on hand. Store it in quart-size plastic containers in your freezer for several months. You might want to make a batch or two of unsalted Roasted Vegetable Broth to keep on hand when an unsalted broth is preferred. MAKES 10 TO 12 CUPS

4 large garlic cloves, halved lengthwise

1 tall celery stalk, leafy top reserved, stalk cut into 2-inch lengths

1 tomato, cut into 1-inch wedges, or 1 cup cherry tomatoes, stems removed

1 large onion, cut into thick slices

1 large carrot, halved lengthwise

1 large parsnip, halved lengthwise

1 turnip, cut into thick slices

8 cremini mushrooms, stems included, halved through the caps

¼ cup extra-virgin olive oil

12 cups water

2 bay leaves

2 leafy sprigs fresh flat-leaf (Italian) parsley

1 sprig fresh thyme

2 teaspoons coarse salt, plus more to taste (optional)

½ teaspoon freshly ground black pepper

1 Preheat the oven to 400°F. Spread the garlic, celery stalk, tomato, onion, carrot, parsnip, turnip, and mushrooms on a large heavy-duty baking sheet. Drizzle with the olive oil. Roast for about 20 minutes. Remove the pan from the oven and carefully turn the vegetables with a wide spatula. Roast until the vegetables are lightly browned, about 20 minutes more, then remove the pan from the oven.

2 Transfer the vegetables to a large pot. Add 1 cup of the water to the baking sheet and scrape the browned bits from the bottom of the pan to deglaze. Carefully tip the pan over the pot to pour in the deglazing water. Add the remaining 11 cups water.

3 Add the reserved celery top, the bay leaves, parsley, thyme, salt (if using), and pepper and bring to a boil. Reduce the heat to medium-low and simmer the broth, uncovered, until reduced to 8 to 10 cups, 1½ to 2 hours.

4 Ladle or pour the broth through a large strainer into a large bowl to remove the vegetables and seasonings. Press down on the vegetables to extract as much flavorful broth as possible. (Discard the vegetables.)

5 To store, divide the broth into 4-cup plastic containers and freeze for 3 months or longer.

Sicilian Fried Eggplant and
Tomato Salad, page 149

SALADS

Pickled Cabbage Slaw

Curdito (sometimes called *curtido*) is a tangy, vinegary slaw typically served with pupusas (page 68), a popular Salvadoran street food that looks like a small, thick pancake. My neighborhood *pupusaria* makes a tangy slaw consisting of only cabbage and white vinegar, but this version is gussied up a bit with rice vinegar, which has a more complex flavor profile then plain white vinegar, and distinctive-tasting Mexican oregano (see page 110). Serve the slaw as a side dish. I like it as an addition to Mexican *torta* (page 77) in place of the Cactus Salad. MAKES 4 SERVINGS

1   small head cabbage, cored, trimmed, and thinly sliced (about 5 cups)

½ cup shredded peeled carrot

½ cup thinly sliced (lengthwise) red onion

2 teaspoons dried Mexican oregano (see page 110) or Greek oregano

1 jalapeño pepper, thinly sliced, or more or less for desired heat

2 teaspoons coarse salt

1 cup unseasoned Japanese rice vinegar or distilled white vinegar

1 Place the sliced cabbage in a large bowl and cover with boiling water. Let stand for 5 minutes; drain and rinse thoroughly with cold water. Wrap the drained cabbage in a kitchen towel and pat dry to absorb the excess water.

2 Combine the cabbage, carrots, onion, oregano, jalapeño, and salt in a large bowl. Pour the vinegar over the top and toss until blended. Serve at once or refrigerate, covered, for later. The slaw will keep for several days, although the texture will soften as it ages.

Shredded Green Salad
with Pomegranate Dressing

Save this recipe for the fall or winter when fresh pomegranates are in the marketplace. Although the seeds are sometimes available in small plastic boxes, I prefer to pop them from the thick membranes of the fruit as the thick skins are peeled away—they are much fresher this way.

MAKES 4 TO 6 SERVINGS

1 head romaine lettuce, trimmed and washed

1 cup thinly sliced scallion (white and green parts)

½ cup finely chopped fresh dill

½ cup finely chopped fresh mint leaves

¼ cup extra-virgin olive oil

2 tablespoons fresh lemon juice

2 tablespoons pomegranate molasses (see page 26)

½ teaspoon coarse salt

⅛ teaspoon freshly ground black pepper

½ cup chopped walnuts

½ cup crumbled feta cheese (see page 62)

½ cup pomegranate seeds

1 Stack the romaine leaves and cut them crosswise into narrow (about ¼-inch) ribbons. You should have about 6 cups. Transfer to a salad bowl and add the scallions, dill, and mint.

2 In a small bowl, whisk together the oil, lemon juice, pomegranate molasses, salt, and pepper until well blended. Pour over the greens and toss to coat. Add the walnuts, cheese, and pomegranate seeds and gently toss to distribute evenly.

Marinated Cucumber Salad

The cucumbers in this salad are first salted before they are marinated, which draws out their water and allows them to crisp in the vinegar-based marinade. This recipe uses rice vinegar and a small amount of toasted sesame oil, but you could create other variations. A Thai version, for example, might use a bit more vinegar and add sugar. The marinated cucumbers will keep, refrigerated, for at least 2 weeks. **MAKES 1 PINT**

2 seedless cucumbers, partially peeled and thinly sliced

2 teaspoons coarse salt

1 cup unseasoned Japanese rice vinegar

2 teaspoons toasted sesame oil (see page 221)

Black sesame seeds, for garnish (optional; see page 60)

1 Layer the cucumbers and salt in a colander. Set a saucer or small plate on top and weight it with a large can or other heavy object. Set the colander over a bowl and let stand for about 1 hour.

2 Drain off all the liquid and squeeze the cucumbers dry in a kitchen towel.

3 Combine the cucumbers, vinegar, and oil in a large bowl and gently fold the ingredients together. Refrigerate until cold and crisp.

4 To serve, lift the cucumbers from the vinegar with tongs and place in a serving dish. Sprinkle lightly with black sesame seeds, if desired.

Cabbage and Apple Salad

A German recipe for sauerkraut salad in my dog-eared and beloved copy of *Jane Grigson's Vegetable Book* was the jumping-off point for this salad. Instead of sauerkraut, I use green cabbage that is allowed to "soften" in boiling water for a few minutes. Apple cider vinegar in the dressing complements the raw apple, as does a lightly flavored vegetable or nut oil, such as grapeseed, hazelnut, or walnut. **MAKES 6 SERVINGS**

1 pound green cabbage, chopped into ¼-inch pieces (about 6 cups)

2 cups diced unpeeled tart, crisp apple, such as Granny Smith, Fuji, or Pink Lady

½ cup coarsely shredded peeled carrot

¼ cup apple cider vinegar

¼ cup lightly flavored vegetable or nut oil, such as grapeseed, hazelnut, or walnut

1 tablespoon finely chopped fresh flat-leaf (Italian) parsley

1 tablespoon finely chopped fresh dill

1 teaspoon coarse salt

1 Place the cabbage in a large bowl and cover with boiling water. Let stand for 5 minutes; drain and rinse thoroughly with cold water. Wrap in a kitchen towel to absorb excess water.

2 In a large bowl, combine the cabbage, apple, carrot, vinegar, oil, parsley, dill, and salt and toss to combine. Serve at once or chill before serving.

Shredded Carrot and Jicama Salad with Lime and Chile Dressing

Jicama is a sweet, crunchy root popular in Mexican and South American recipes. To prepare it, cut the bulb into wedges and then peel the tan skin, which can sometimes be thick, with a small paring knife. Look for jicama in the produce section of most supermarkets. Its juicy flesh makes a delicious snack sliced and sprinkled with salt and ground chile peppers.

MAKES 4 SERVINGS

- 1 pound jicama, cut into wedges and peeled
- 3 or 4 carrots, trimmed and peeled
- 2 scallions, thinly sliced (white and green parts)
- ¼ cup chopped fresh cilantro
- ⅓ cup fresh lime juice
- ⅓ cup vegetable oil
- ½ teaspoon coarse salt
- ⅛ teaspoon cayenne pepper or ¼ teaspoon finely chopped chipotle in adobo sauce (see box)

1 Using the wide holes of a box grater or the shredding blade of a food processor, coarsely shred the jicama and carrots. In a salad bowl, combine the jicama, carrots, scallions, and cilantro.

2 In a small bowl, whisk together the lime juice, oil, salt, and cayenne. Pour over the salad and toss to blend.

Chipotle in Adobo Sauce

Chipotles are dried smoked jalapeño peppers. They are typically packed in small cans and preserved in a vinegary sauce called adobo sauce. Their popularity comes from their beloved smoky taste and intense heat—beware, they are hot—which is balanced by a complex, almost chocolaty taste. Because they are generally used in small amounts, one way to preserve the rest of the can is to remove and discard the stems from the chiles, puree the chiles and the adobo sauce in a food processor, and freeze by teaspoonfuls on a piece of foil until solid. Then peel off the blobs of frozen chipotle, transfer to a resealable bag, and keep in the freezer until needed.

Vegetarian Kimchi

Making kimchi from scratch occurred to me when Joe Yonan suggested, in his excellent cookbook *Eat Your Vegetables*, to make a vegetarian version with miso instead of fish sauce. Brilliant! There is nothing hard about making this unique Korean condiment, although you may need to seek out a well-stocked Asian market for some of the ingredients, including the unique ground red pepper—a must—called gochugaru (see page 134). Adding nori contributes a hint of the sea that goes missing when fish sauce is omitted. I also like the rounded taste that comes from the addition of sesame oil and sesame seeds. **MAKES 1 PINT**

1 pound napa cabbage, quartered lengthwise, cored, and cut crosswise into 1-inch slices

¼ cup coarse salt

¼ cup water

2 to 3 tablespoons gochugaru, depending on desired heat

2 tablespoons grated garlic

1 tablespoon grated peeled fresh ginger

1 tablespoon red miso paste

¼ cup thinly sliced scallion (green and white parts, cut on the diagonal)

2 tablespoons thin slivers nori (Japanese seaweed; optional)

2 teaspoons tan sesame seeds (see page 60)

2 teaspoons toasted sesame oil (see page 221)

1 Place the cabbage in a large bowl and add the salt. Massage the cabbage, squeezing it in your hands until the leaves appear bruised, about 2 minutes. Cover with cold water. Place a plate on top and weight it with a heavy can. Let stand for 2 hours. Drain off the water, then rinse the cabbage in two or three changes of clean water. Place the cabbage in a kitchen towel and blot dry.

2 In a small bowl, combine the water, the gochugaru, garlic, ginger, and miso. Stir into a paste. Pour the paste over the cabbage and massage with your hands until blended. Add the scallions, nori (if using), sesame seeds, and sesame oil. Squeeze with your hands to combine.

3 Firmly pack the mixture into a pint jar, pressing down so that the liquid covers the solids. If it all doesn't fit in one jar, place any extra in a smaller jar. Let stand in a dark spot, at room temperature, turning the jar over at least once a day so the flavors will be evenly distributed. After 3 or 4 days the mixture will begin to bubble, or ferment. Once the kimchi begins to ferment, open the jar every other day and press down on the cabbage with the back of a spoon so it remains covered with the liquid. When it is fermented enough for your taste (usually 5 to 7 days), refrigerate the kimchi, but let it stand for at least 1 week more in the refrigerator before using.

Gochugaru

A dried ground Korean chile pepper with a sweet, smoky taste, gochugaru has a layered spiciness that doesn't burn. The heat can be moderate to intense depending on the amount added to a recipe. The brand I buy at my local Asian supermarket comes in a rectangular red tub, but you will also find it in bags or bottles.

Carrots Pickled in Soy and Rice Vinegar

A simple pickle of matchstick carrots makes a bright salad or side dish. I like it both as a topping for a mixed green salad, using the marinating liquid as the dressing, and as a topping for a bowl of sushi rice along with Glazed Eggplant (page 286) and Marinated Cucumber Salad (page 128). This salad is also delicious made with shredded cabbage and carrots, as described in the variation that follows. MAKES 4 SERVINGS

2 large carrots, peeled and cut into 2-inch-long matchsticks

1 teaspoon coarse salt

⅓ cup unseasoned Japanese rice vinegar

3 tablespoons mirin (sweet rice wine)

2 tablespoons tamari (see page 44)

½ teaspoon toasted sesame oil (optional; see page 221)

½ teaspoon tan sesame seeds (see page 60)

1 Toss the carrots in a bowl with the salt. Cover and let stand for about 1 hour, or until limp. Rinse the carrots under running water, then place in a bowl filled with cold water and swish them around the bowl for 20 seconds. Drain and spread on a kitchen towel to dry.

2 Whisk together the vinegar, mirin, tamari, and sesame oil (if using) in a medium bowl. Add the carrots and toss to combine. Cover and marinate either in the refrigerator or at room temperature for at least 2 hours. Serve chilled or at room temperature. Sprinkle with the sesame seeds before serving.

Variation
CABBAGE PICKLED IN SOY AND RICE VINEGAR

For the matchstick carrots, substitute 4 cups thinly shredded cabbage and ¼ cup coarsely shredded carrot.

Spinach and Fuyu Persimmon Salad with Sesame-Mirin Dressing

Fuyu are the small, crunchy, sweet, tomato-shaped variety of persimmon, and a world apart from the heart-shaped soft but tannic Hachiya variety. In the winter months, when flavorful tomatoes are not readily available, thin wedges of Fuyu persimmon add color and crunch to salads. Mirin, a sweet wine made from glutinous rice, is a staple in Japanese kitchens and finds its way into marinades, glazes, dressings, and all-purpose seasoning. Here, its sweetness balances the salt in the tamari or soy sauce. If persimmons are not available, substitute yellow tomatoes. **MAKES 4 SERVINGS**

1 tablespoon tamari or soy sauce (see page 44)

1 tablespoon mirin (sweet rice wine)

1 tablespoon neutral-flavored vegetable oil

½ teaspoon toasted sesame oil (see page 221)

½ teaspoon grated peeled fresh ginger

¼ teaspoon grated garlic

1 bunch (about 12 ounces) large-leaf spinach, long stems trimmed, rinsed and dried, or 1½ bags (10 ounces each) baby spinach, rinsed and dried

1 Fuyu persimmon, trimmed, thinly sliced, slices halved, or 1 yellow tomato, sliced into wedges

½ cup thinly sliced small Persian cucumber or halved slices seedless cucumber

½ teaspoon tan sesame seeds (see page 60)

1 In a salad bowl, whisk together the tamari, mirin, oils, ginger, and garlic until well blended.

2 Add the spinach, persimmon, and cucumbers and toss to coat. Sprinkle with the sesame seeds.

Jicama, Pineapple, and Orange Salad

You can make this especially pretty and refreshing salad with winter or summer produce. To save time, you can use canned pineapple chunks instead of fresh. I find it easier to peel jicama if I first cut it into quarters and then use a paring knife to remove the coarse skin. Be sure to cut the jicama into bite-size pieces just a bit smaller than the pineapple chunks.

MAKES 4 SERVINGS

2 large navel oranges, peel and white pith removed

1 can (20 ounces) pineapple chunks, drained, or 2 cups fresh pineapple cut into ¼-inch cubes

1 pound jicama, peeled and cut into ¼-inch pieces (about 2 cups)

¼ cup coarsely chopped fresh cilantro leaves

¼ cup thinly sliced scallion (white and green parts)

¼ cup minced red bell pepper or pomegranate seeds (optional)

1 teaspoon minced jalapeño pepper, or more to taste

½ teaspoon coarse salt

¼ cup fresh lime juice

1 Cut the orange into ½-inch-thick slices, and then cut the slices into ½-inch chunks. You should have about 2 cups.

2 In a large bowl, combine the oranges, pineapple, jicama, cilantro, scallions, bell pepper (if using), jalapeño, and salt; gently toss to combine. Sprinkle with the lime juice. Refrigerate until chilled, about 30 minutes, before serving.

Tomato, Cucumber, and Green Bean Salad with Walnut Dressing

In this summer salad, the walnuts are ground with garlic to make a creamy dressing before they are blended with the olive oil and vinegar. This simple but distinctive dressing, which I first tasted at a Georgian restaurant in New York City, is easily adapted to your repertoire of summer salads.

MAKES 4 SERVINGS

⅓ cup broken walnut pieces

1 garlic clove, chopped

1 teaspoon coarse salt

3 tablespoons extra-virgin olive oil

3 tablespoons red wine vinegar

½ pound green beans, stem ends trimmed, cut into 1-inch lengths

2 large firm ripe plum tomatoes, quartered and cut crosswise into ½-inch pieces

½ cup thinly sliced (lengthwise) red onion

½ cucumber, peeled, seeded, halved lengthwise, and cut into ¼-inch slices

¼ cup coarsely chopped fresh cilantro

¼ cup coarsely chopped fresh dill

¼ cup coarsely chopped fresh mint

1 Combine the walnuts, garlic, and salt in a food processor and blend until finely ground. If preferred, the walnuts, garlic, and salt can be pounded into a paste with a mortar and pestle. Combine the walnut mixture, oil, and vinegar in a salad bowl and whisk until blended.

2 Cook the green beans in boiling salted water until crisp-tender, 4 to 6 minutes. Drain well, rinse with cold water, spread on a dish towel, and pat dry.

3 Add the green beans, tomatoes, onion, cucumber, and herbs to the walnut dressing and toss to blend.

Tomato, Onion, and Cilantro Salad

What fascinates me about this Afghani *salata* is the absence of oil. Instead, it is dressed with fresh lemon juice stirred with garlic and salt. The bright flavors of the large cubes of raw vegetables simply dressed with fresh lemon juice bring a nice counterpoint when spooned onto a bowl of cooked brown rice, tender cooked cannellini or black beans, or a bowl of cooked green beans or broccoli. **MAKES 4 SERVINGS**

3 tablespoons fresh lemon juice

1 small garlic clove, grated or minced

½ teaspoon coarse salt

2 medium tomatoes, quartered, then halved crosswise

1 small cucumber, diced into ½-inch pieces

½ sweet onion, diced into ½-inch pieces (about 1 cup)

1 jalapeño or other chile pepper, seeds removed, thinly sliced

¼ cup lightly packed coarsely chopped fresh cilantro leaves and tender stems

In a large bowl, stir together the lemon juice, garlic, and salt until well blended and the salt is dissolved. Add the tomatoes, cucumber, onion, jalapeño, and cilantro and gently toss until evenly coated with the dressing. Serve at room temperature.

Tomato and Poblano Chile Salad with Toasted Pepitas

Poblano chiles can vary from sweet to mildly hot. I suggest buying a couple and tasting before adding to the salad so you can gauge the intensity of the heat. Create variations by adding diced avocado or fresh raw corn cut from the cob or slivers of sweet white onion, or by using a medley of yellow, red, and green tomatoes. **MAKES 4 SERVINGS**

1½ pounds ripe tomatoes, cored, cut into ½-inch wedges

1 teaspoon coarse salt

1 poblano chile, cut into thin rings, stem and seeds discarded

½ cup coarsely chopped fresh cilantro leaves and tender stems

2 tablespoons extra-virgin olive oil

2 tablespoons fresh lime juice

2 tablespoons hulled pepitas (pumpkin seeds; see box)

Pepitas

Pepitas are pumpkin seeds that are oval and flat, light green in color (when shelled; sometimes the shells are white and crunchy), and used often in Mexican cooking. The shell is typically soft and edible, but they are also available shelled. They are sold roasted or raw, salted or unsalted in bags, bulk, or boxes. Store them in the freezer or refrigerator to discourage rancidity.

1 Place the tomatoes in a large salad bowl and sprinkle with the salt. Add the poblano, cilantro, oil, and lime juice and gently toss.

2 Heat a small heavy skillet over medium-high heat until hot enough to sizzle a drop of water. Add the pepitas and toast, stirring, until they turn a shade darker, about 3 minutes. Let cool and then sprinkle over the salad.

Carrot Salad with
Toasted Cumin Dressing

A Moroccan meze, or first course, is usually a medley of well-seasoned cooked vegetables served at room temperature. Small servings are heaped onto plates and eaten with pieces of pita. This cooked carrot salad is just one example of a wide repertoire. Serve it with Swiss Chard Salad with Moroccan Preserved Lemons (page 158) and Cooked Red Pepper, Zucchini, and Eggplant Salad with Mint (page 154) to make a full course.

MAKES 4 SERVINGS

12 ounces large carrots, peeled, halved lengthwise, and cut into ½-inch pieces on the diagonal (about 3 cups)

½ cup water

2 garlic cloves, crushed with the side of a knife

¼ teaspoon coriander seeds

¼ teaspoon crushed red pepper flakes

1½ teaspoons ground cumin

2 tablespoons fresh lemon juice

2 tablespoons extra-virgin olive oil

½ teaspoon coarse salt

¼ teaspoon freshly ground black pepper

¼ cup halved pitted brine-cured green olives

1 Combine the carrots, water, garlic, coriander, and red pepper flakes in a medium saucepan. Bring to a boil and cook, covered, over medium-low heat until the carrots are crisp-tender, 4 to 6 minutes. Uncover and cook until the water has evaporated, about 1 minute.

2 Stir the cumin in a small heavy skillet over low heat until fragrant, about 1 minute. Remove from the heat. Add the lemon juice, oil, salt, and black pepper and whisk until blended. Pour the dressing over the cooked carrots and let cool to room temperature. Sprinkle with the olives. Serve either chilled or at room temperature.

Sicilian Fried Eggplant and Tomato Salad

This is a perfect salad for late-summer ripe tomatoes and eggplants. The fried eggplant, although it takes a few extra minutes to prepare, is a delectable treat. Try it tossed with hot pasta. **MAKES 4 SERVINGS**

1½ to 2 pounds eggplant, trimmed and peeled

2 tablespoons coarse salt

¼ cup extra-virgin olive oil, plus more for frying

2 cups diced (¼-inch pieces) firm ripe plum tomatoes

1 cup diced celery

⅓ cup finely chopped fresh flat-leaf (Italian) parsley

½ cup diced green or red bell pepper

¼ cup chopped pitted brine-cured black or green olives

1 tablespoon capers, rinsed and blotted dry

¼ cup red wine vinegar

1 garlic clove, grated

¼ teaspoon freshly ground black pepper, or to taste

½ cup chopped or diced Pecorino Romano cheese

1 Cut the eggplant into ¼- to ⅓-inch-thick rounds. Stack and cut crosswise into ¼-inch-wide "sticks." Toss with the salt and place in a colander set over a bowl or deep platter. Place a plate, just smaller than the circumference of the colander, on top of the eggplant and weight it down with a can of tomatoes or some other heavy object. Let stand for at least 1 hour. Rinse off the salt and spread the eggplant on a kitchen towel. Wrap the towel around the eggplant and squeeze to release the excess moisture.

2 Heat about 1 inch of olive oil (or use a combination of olive oil and vegetable oil) in a deep skillet until hot enough to sizzle and brown a crust of bread. Fry the eggplant in three batches to avoid crowding the pan, adjusting the heat as needed to keep the eggplant sizzling and gently stirring with a long fork, until dark brown, 8 to 10 minutes. Use a slotted spoon to transfer the browned eggplant to a strainer set over a bowl to drain as you finish each batch.

3 Place the eggplant in a large bowl and add the tomatoes, celery, parsley, bell pepper, olives, and capers. In a small bowl, whisk together the vinegar, remaining ¼ cup olive oil, garlic, and black pepper. Add to the salad and toss. Sprinkle the cheese on top and serve.

Warm Potato Salad with Green Olive Vinaigrette

Potato salads are universally appealing, especially this interpretation from the Italian kitchen. You can use almost any green olive for this salad, but I prefer the meaty, mild-tasting, bright green Castelvetrano olive, named for the town in Sicily. MAKES 4 SERVINGS

½ cup diced (¼-inch pieces) red onion

1 to 1½ pounds all-purpose white or Yukon gold potatoes

3 tablespoons fruity extra-virgin olive oil

2 tablespoons aged red wine vinegar

1 teaspoon coarse salt

½ teaspoon dried oregano

⅛ teaspoon freshly ground black pepper

½ cup Italian green olives plus 8 to 10, whole, for garnish

½ cup sliced (¼-inch pieces) celery

2 tablespoons chopped celery leaves

1 tablespoon capers, rinsed and dried

1 Place the onion in a small bowl and cover with cold water. Let stand for about 20 minutes. Drain and pat dry. (Soaking the onion will take out some of the volatile oils and mellow the flavor of the onion.)

2 Place the potatoes in a medium saucepan and cover with water. Bring to a boil and cook, covered, until tender when pierced with a skewer, 20 to 25 minutes depending on their size. Drain.

3 Meanwhile, whisk together the oil, vinegar, salt, oregano, and pepper in a small bowl. Press a large knife down on the olives to crush and loosen the pits. Discard the pits and chop the olives into small pieces. Add the chopped olives to the dressing and mash together with the back of a spoon.

4 While the potatoes are still warm but cool enough to handle, use a paring knife to pull off the skins and dice the potatoes into ¼- to ½-inch pieces.

5 In a salad bowl, combine the warm potatoes, onion, celery, celery leaves, and capers. Add the dressing and gently toss to blend. Garnish with the remaining whole olives, and serve warm.

Cold Potato, Beet, Carrot, and Pea Salad with Dill

Bright green peas are tossed in with the purple beets and orange carrots in this multicolored salad. But because the vinaigrette dressing quickly transforms the peas from brilliant green to drab, add them just before serving. Either chilled or at room temperature, this salad can be served as a side dish or a main course, spooned onto a platter and garnished with tomato wedges, cucumber slices, and halved hard-cooked eggs. **MAKES 4 SERVINGS**

1 cup coarsely chopped red onion

2 medium beets, tops trimmed (about 8 ounces)

3 medium potatoes (about 12 ounces)

2 medium carrots, peeled, cut into ½-inch pieces (about 1 cup)

½ cup chopped dill pickles

¼ cup chopped fresh dill

¼ cup extra-virgin olive oil

¼ cup red wine vinegar

2 teaspoons prepared whole-grain mustard

½ teaspoon coarse salt

¼ teaspoon freshly ground black pepper

½ cup frozen petite green peas, thawed

1 Place the onion in a small bowl and cover with cold water. Let stand for about 20 minutes. Drain and pat dry. (Soaking the onion will take out some of the volatile oils and mellow the flavor of the onion.)

2 Halve the beets and place in a vegetable steamer set over boiling water. Steam, covered, until tender when pierced with the tip of a knife, 20 to 35 minutes. Let cool. Use a paring knife to pull off the loosened skins. Cut the beets into ½-inch cubes.

3 Meanwhile, place the potatoes in a saucepan and cover with water. Bring to a boil and cook, covered, until almost tender, about 15 minutes. Add the carrots and cook until the potatoes are ready and the carrots are crisp-tender, about 5 minutes more. Drain and let cool. With a paring knife, peel the loosened skins from the potatoes and then cut them into ½-inch cubes.

4 In a large salad bowl, combine the beets, potatoes, carrots, pickles, onions, and half of the dill.

5 In a small bowl, whisk together the olive oil, vinegar, mustard, salt, and pepper until blended. Pour over the vegetables and gently fold to combine.

6 Serve at room temperature or chilled. Just before serving, spoon the peas over the salad and sprinkle with the remaining dill.

Cooked Red Pepper, Zucchini, and Eggplant Salad with Mint

I like to make this Moroccan salad in my wok-shaped skillet, but any large skillet will do. Serve the salad at room temperature or chilled, with plenty of warm pita to scoop it from plate to mouth, in the style of Morocco.

MAKES 4 SERVINGS

- 1 pound tomatoes, blossom ends cut with an X
- ¼ cup extra-virgin olive oil
- 1 small (about 12 ounces) eggplant, peeled and cut into 1-inch chunks
- ½ teaspoon coarse salt

  Freshly ground black pepper
- 1 red bell pepper, stem and seeds removed, cut into ¾-inch pieces
- 1 medium zucchini, trimmed, halved lengthwise, and sliced ½ inch thick
- 2 tablespoons finely chopped fresh mint or 1 tablespoon dried mint
- 2 tablespoons red wine vinegar

1 Bring a saucepan half filled with water to a boil. Add the tomatoes, stem sides down, and boil until the skins begin to peel away from the X, 2 to 3 minutes. Use a slotted spoon to transfer the tomatoes from the water to a plate; let stand until cool. Peel off the skins, and cut out and discard the stem ends. Squeeze the tomatoes into a strainer set over a small bowl. Strain the juices into the bowl and discard the seeds. Coarsely chop the tomato flesh. Add the chopped flesh to the bowl with the juices and set aside.

2 Heat the oil in a skillet over medium-high heat until hot enough to sizzle a piece of eggplant. Add the eggplant and stir-fry until lightly browned, about 5 minutes. Add the salt and a generous grinding of black pepper.

3 Add the bell pepper and stir-fry until lightly browned, about 5 minutes. Add the tomatoes and their juice, zucchini, and mint and cook, stirring, until the tomato juices are reduced and thickened and the vegetables are soft, about 10 minutes.

4 Remove the skillet from the heat and stir in the vinegar. Serve chilled or at room temperature.

Eggplant Salad

For this salad, Japanese use the long, sweet, seed-free slender Japanese eggplants. In this recipe they are seared in a skillet and then briefly cooked in a piquant rice vinegar–based dressing. You can serve the salad either chilled or at room temperature. MAKES 4 SERVINGS

½ cup unseasoned Japanese rice vinegar

2 teaspoons shoyu, tamari, or soy sauce (see page 44)

1 teaspoon toasted sesame oil (see page 221)

1 teaspoon grated peeled fresh ginger

¼ teaspoon grated garlic

2 tablespoons vegetable oil

3 Japanese eggplants (about 1½ pounds), trimmed and halved lengthwise

2 tablespoons finely chopped red bell pepper

1 tablespoon thinly sliced scallion (green tops only)

1 In a small bowl, whisk together the rice vinegar, shoyu, sesame oil, ginger, and garlic.

2 Heat a skillet large enough to hold the eggplant halves in a single layer over high heat until hot enough to evaporate a drop of water. Add the vegetable oil and heat for a few seconds, or until shimmering. Add the eggplant, cut sides down, and reduce the heat to medium-high. Cook the eggplant until golden brown on one side, about 5 minutes, then turn and cook until the other side is browned, about 5 minutes.

3 Add the dressing, turning the eggplant to coat, and cook until the eggplant is tender, about 2 minutes more. Transfer the eggplant, cut side up, to a platter and spoon the warm dressing on top, distributing evenly. Sprinkle with the bell pepper and scallions. Serve at room temperature or chilled.

Swiss Chard Salad with Moroccan Preserved Lemons

Leftovers of this Swiss chard "salad" are delicious folded into pita and eaten as a sandwich. The cooked Swiss chard is also wonderful served as a topping for Crostini (page 23), albeit more Italian than Middle Eastern. For an appetizer plate or light meal with pita bread, it's good with the Carrot Salad with Toasted Cumin Dressing (page 146) and the Cooked Red Pepper, Zucchini, and Eggplant Salad with Mint (page 154). **MAKES 4 SERVINGS**

2 large bunches (about 1½ pounds) Swiss chard

2 garlic cloves, chopped or grated

½ teaspoon coarse salt

2 tablespoons extra-virgin olive oil

2 teaspoons sweet paprika

Pinch of crushed red pepper flakes

1 tablespoon finely chopped rind from Moroccan Preserved Lemons (page 305)

1 Strip the leaves from the Swiss chard (reserve the stems for soup or another use). Tear the leaves into 1- to 2-inch pieces. You should have about 8 cups, lightly packed.

2 Mash the chopped garlic and salt using a mortar and pestle to form a paste. If you don't have a mortar and pestle, mash the grated garlic and salt together on a saucer with the back of a fork.

3 Heat the oil and the garlic mixture in a large skillet over medium-low heat just until the garlic begins to sizzle. Stir in the paprika and red pepper flakes.

4 Gradually add the Swiss chard to the skillet a few handfuls at a time, tossing with tongs. When all the Swiss chard has been added, cook, tossing, over medium heat until the Swiss chard is wilted and tender, about 5 minutes.

5 Remove from the heat, sprinkle the chard with the preserved lemon rind, and then let cool to room temperature before serving.

Cactus Salad

Nopales, eaten as a vegetable all over Mexico, taste like a watermelon but with the texture of a peach. They are the paddles from the prickly pear cactus. Nopales are added to cooked dishes or used in salads. If you have access to fresh cactus (called paddles), or nopales, the directions below will guide you in their preparation. If you decide not to venture into fresh nopales territory, you can buy good-quality jarred nopales wherever Mexican groceries are sold. Cactus Salad can be served as a side dish salad, as a topping for tortillas as you would use guacamole, or as a filling for Mexican *torta* (page 77). **MAKES 4 SERVINGS**

- 2 medium (approximately 6 x 4 inches) fresh cactus paddles (about 12 ounces) or 1 jar (12 ounces) nopalitos, or cactus pieces, drained, rinsed well, and patted dry
- 1 plum tomato
- ¼ cup mayonnaise
- 2 tablespoons minced white onion
- 1 tablespoon distilled white vinegar
- 1 tablespoon finely chopped fresh cilantro
- 1 teaspoon finely chopped jalapeño pepper, or more to taste
- ½ teaspoon coarse salt

1 If using fresh cactus paddles, wear thick rubber gloves to protect your hands. With a paring knife, trim about ¼ inch from the edges of the paddles and remove the spiny nodes from both sides. Cut the cactus crosswise into ¼-inch strips.

2 Bring a large saucepan three quarters filled with water to a boil. Add the cactus and boil until tender, 15 to 20 minutes. Drain and rinse well under cold water. Pat the cactus dry with a kitchen towel and dice into ¼-inch pieces. Alternatively, the whole cactus paddles can be grilled instead of boiled. To grill, preheat the grill until very hot, score the surface of the cactus at 2-inch intervals, and brush with vegetable oil. Reduce the heat of the grill to medium and cook the cactus, turning occasionally, until tender, about 15 minutes. If using jarred nopales, simply cut the cactus into ¼-inch pieces.

3 Halve the tomato lengthwise and scoop out and discard the seeds and pulp. Cut the tomato flesh into ¼-inch pieces.

4 In a large bowl, combine the cactus, tomato, mayonnaise, onion, vinegar, cilantro, jalapeño, and salt. Refrigerate until ready to serve. Serve chilled.

Warm Lentil Salad with Walnuts

There are many versions of lentil salad in the French repertoire. This one is delicious made with the tiny green peppery French lentil called du Puy, but the brown common lentil works well, too. I use walnut oil in the dressing because I like its mellow, mildly nutty flavor, which complements the lentils and walnuts. If you prefer olive oil, use a mild, not overly fruity, one that won't overwhelm the other ingredients. The salad is meant to be served warm or at room temperature, although refrigerated leftovers are excellent. A side of green beans or other green vegetable makes it a meal.

MAKES 4 SERVINGS

1½ cups lentils, preferably French du Puy

1½ teaspoons coarse salt

1 thick slice onion

1 bay leaf

1 cinnamon stick

3 tablespoons dried currants

½ cup chopped walnuts

¼ cup finely chopped shallot

¼ cup finely chopped fresh flat-leaf (Italian) or curly-leaf parsley

¼ cup walnut oil or a mild olive oil

3 tablespoons red wine vinegar

1 teaspoon whole-grain mustard

Freshly ground black pepper

1 Bring a large pot half filled with water to a boil. Add the lentils, 1 teaspoon of the salt, onion, bay leaf, and cinnamon stick. Boil gently, stirring occasionally, over medium-low heat, until the lentils are tender, 15 to 25 minutes, or more if needed, depending on their type and age.

2 Ladle ¼ cup of the simmering cooking liquid into a small bowl and add the currants. Plump in the hot water for 10 minutes and then drain.

3 Meanwhile, preheat the oven to 350°F. Spread the walnuts in a small baking dish and bake until lightly toasted, about 15 minutes. Let cool.

4 Drain the cooked lentils and discard the onion, bay leaf, and cinnamon stick. Transfer the lentils to a large serving bowl and add the currants, shallots, and parsley.

5 In a small saucepan, whisk together the oil, vinegar, mustard, remaining ½ teaspoon salt, and a grinding of pepper over low heat until warmed. Add to the lentils and gently toss to combine. Sprinkle the walnuts on top and serve either while still warm or at room temperature.

Chickpea and Parsley Salad

Best known as the dried legume in hummus, chickpeas are left whole here and tossed with lots of parsley. You can use dried chickpeas that have been reconstituted and cooked until tender or their canned counterpart, but because I prefer the texture and rich creamy taste of chickpeas cooked from dried, I give those instructions in the recipe. Chopping so much parsley might seem like a daunting task, but unless you are vigilant, the food processor will turn it into mush. **A tip:** Gather the parsley into little bouquets and trim the long thicker stems. Chopping a small bouquet at a time, chop through the leafy tops. For this salad, I prefer curly-leaf parsley to Italian parsley, whose leaves are often thicker and a little tough in comparison. MAKES 4 SERVINGS

1 cup dried chickpeas or 2 cans (15 ounces each) chickpeas, rinsed and drained

1 onion wedge (for dried chickpeas)

1 bay leaf (for dried chickpeas)

1 garlic clove, bruised with the side of a knife (for dried chickpeas)

¼ cup extra-virgin olive oil

3 tablespoons fresh lemon juice

2 tablespoons tahini (see page 41)

½ teaspoon coarse salt

⅛ teaspoon grated garlic

2 cups finely chopped fresh curly-leaf parsley, thick stems trimmed

¼ cup thinly sliced scallion

1 If using dried chickpeas: Place the chickpeas in a bowl and add water to cover. Soak for at least 6 hours or overnight.

2 Preheat the oven to 350°F. Drain and discard the water from the soaked chickpeas. Transfer the chickpeas to an ovenproof casserole; add the onion, bay leaf, bruised garlic, and enough water to cover the chickpeas. Cover tightly with foil or a lid and bake until the chickpeas are tender, adding more water if needed, 1 to 1½ hours depending on the age of the chickpeas. Drain and discard the onion, bay leaf, and garlic. You should have about 3 cups cooked chickpeas.

3 In a large bowl, whisk together the oil, lemon juice, tahini, salt, and grated garlic until blended. Add the chickpeas, parsley, and scallions. Gently fold until combined. Serve chilled or at room temperature.

Tuscan Rice Salad

Rice salad presents a canvas for endless variations. I am partial to this version, which incorporates cooked scrambled eggs along with a rainbow of diced vegetables. But it's the grated Parmigiano-Reggiano that truly sets this salad apart. **MAKES 4 SERVINGS**

2 cups water

1 cup medium- or long-grain white rice

Coarse salt

3 large eggs, beaten

¼ cup plus 2 teaspoons extra-virgin olive oil

1 small garlic clove, grated

Freshly ground black pepper

⅓ cup fresh lemon juice

½ cup diced (⅛-inch pieces) peeled carrot

½ cup frozen petite peas, thawed

¼ cup diced (⅛-inch pieces) red onion

2 tablespoons torn fresh basil leaves

2 tablespoons finely chopped fresh flat-leaf (Italian) parsley

2 tablespoons grated Parmigiano-Reggiano

¼ cup shaved curls of Parmigiano-Reggiano, cut with a vegetable peeler from a wedge of cheese

1 Bring the water to a boil in a medium pot. Stir in the rice and 1 teaspoon of salt. Cook, covered, over medium heat, without stirring, until the water is absorbed and the rice is tender, about 15 minutes. Let stand, covered, until cooled.

2 In a medium bowl, whisk together the eggs, 1 teaspoon of the oil, and the garlic. Heat a small, heavy skillet over medium-low heat until hot enough to sizzle a drop of water. Add 1 teaspoon of the oil, tilting the pan to coat evenly. Add the eggs and cook, stirring with a heatproof rubber spatula as the eggs begin to set, until the eggs are scrambled into large clumps. Remove from the heat and sprinkle lightly with salt and a grinding of black pepper.

3 In a large serving bowl, whisk together the lemon juice, remaining ¼ cup oil, a pinch of salt, and a grinding of black pepper. Add the rice, scrambled eggs, carrots, peas, onion, basil, parsley, and grated cheese. Gently toss until blended. Garnish with the curls of Parmigiano-Reggiano. Serve warm or at room temperature.

Warm Rice Salad with Green Olives and Cheese

This pretty salad tosses warm rice with lightly sautéed celery and is made lively with salty cracked green olives and a popular Greek cheese called kasseri (see page 265). If you can't find kasseri, use a mild Italian provolone. If you prefer, make the salad with medium-grain brown rice instead of white. I adapted the recipe from one by Diane Kochilas, a longtime friend and the writer of extraordinary Greek cookbooks. **MAKES 4 SERVINGS**

2 cups water (or 2¾ cups if using brown rice)

1 cup medium-grain white rice, such as Calrose or Arborio, or brown rice, such as Lundberg

1 teaspoon coarse salt

3 tablespoons extra-virgin olive oil

1 cup diced (⅛-inch pieces) celery, including a few leaves

½ teaspoon coarsely ground coriander seeds (optional)

1 garlic clove, finely chopped

½ cup brine-cured cracked Greek olives, pitted and coarsely chopped

½ cup diced (⅛-inch pieces) kasseri (see page 265) or Italian provolone cheese

2 tablespoons fresh lemon juice, plus more to taste

1 teaspoon grated lemon zest

1 In a large saucepan, bring the water to a boil. Stir in the rice and salt. Cover and cook over medium-low heat, without stirring, until the water is absorbed and the rice is tender, about 15 minutes for white rice and 55 minutes for brown. Remove from the heat.

2 While the rice is cooking, heat 2 tablespoons of the oil in a medium skillet until hot enough to sizzle a piece of celery. Turn the heat to low and stir in the celery and coriander seeds, if using. Cook, stirring, until the celery is translucent, about 3 minutes. Stir in the garlic and cook, stirring, for about 20 seconds. Do not brown. Remove from the heat.

3 In a large bowl, combine the warm rice, celery mixture, olives, cheese, lemon juice, lemon zest, and remaining 1 tablespoon oil. Toss and serve warm or at room temperature.

Japanese Brown Rice Salad

In this simple brown rice salad I use hijiki, a highly nutritious twiggy black marine algae that grows along the coast of Japan. Its taste is reminiscent of the sea. It is sold dried in Asian markets in small cellophane packets. It needs to be soaked for a short time and then boiled and cooled before using. The dressing is a simple rice vinegar and vegetable oil mixture with a bit of fresh ginger for an extra kick. **MAKES 4 SERVINGS**

1⅓ cups medium-grain brown rice

1 tablespoon coarse salt

¼ cup (about ¼ ounce) dried hijiki

½ cup shredded peeled carrot

¼ cup thinly sliced scallion (green parts only)

¼ cup diced (⅛-inch pieces) seedless cucumber

¼ cup vegetable oil

¼ cup unseasoned Japanese rice vinegar

1 teaspoon toasted sesame oil (see page 221)

1 teaspoon tamari or soy sauce (see page 44)

1 teaspoon grated peeled fresh ginger

1 tablespoon tan sesame seeds (see page 60)

1 Bring a large pot of water to a boil. Stir in the rice and salt. Cook, uncovered, in gently boiling water, until the rice is tender, 45 to 55 minutes. Drain and rinse with cold water.

2 While the rice is cooking, place the hijiki in a small bowl and cover with cold water. Let stand for 30 minutes. Drain. Bring a medium pot of water to a boil and add the hijiki. Boil the hijiki for 20 minutes. Drain and rinse thoroughly. Spread on a clean kitchen towel, fold the towel over the hijiki, and pat to remove excess moisture. Measure out ½ cup of the reconstituted hijiki. Reserve any remaining in a container in the refrigerator for 2 or 3 days. (It is excellent stirred into broth or added to salads.)

3 Combine the rice, hijiki, carrot, scallion, and cucumber in a salad bowl.

4 In a small bowl, whisk together the vegetable oil, vinegar, sesame oil, tamari, and ginger until blended. Add to the rice and toss to coat. Sprinkle with the sesame seeds and serve at room temperature.

MAIN DISH SALADS
Tabbouleh

Tabbouleh is considered by many Lebanese to be their national dish. I have come to love a version where the green herbs—in this case, the parsley and mint—not the bulgur, are the main ingredients. The herbs impart a bright taste and wonderfully addictive fragrance. **MAKES 4 SERVINGS**

⅓ cup fine, medium, or coarse tan-colored bulgur (see page 170)

½ cup boiling water

3 large ripe tomatoes, trimmed

1 or 2 bunches fresh curly-leaf parsley, washed and shaken dry

1 or 2 bunches fresh mint

¼ cup extra-virgin olive oil

2 tablespoons fresh lemon juice

½ teaspoon coarse salt

1 cup thinly sliced scallion (white and green parts)

1 Place the bulgur in a small bowl and add the boiling water. Cover and let stand until fluffy, 20 to 30 minutes. Taste the bulgur; it should be slightly chewy. If there is unabsorbed water in the bowl, transfer the bulgur to a strainer and press gently with the back of a spoon. Discard the water and transfer the bulgur to a small bowl.

2 Cut the stem end from the tomatoes. Place a strainer over a bowl and squeeze the juice and seeds from the tomatoes through the strainer. Press the seeds and pulp in the strainer with the back of a spoon to extract as much tomato juice as possible. Discard the seeds and reserve the tomato juice. Carefully cut the tomatoes into ¼-inch pieces. You should have about 3 cups.

3 Gather the parsley into a bundle and cut off and discard the long thick stems. Finely chop the leaves and tender stems with a large chef's knife. It's best to chop the herbs by hand. A food processor will turn the parsley to mush. Continue chopping until you have at least 2 cups. Repeat with the mint until the chopped mint measures 1 cup.

4 Add the oil, lemon juice, salt, and 2 tablespoons of the reserved tomato juice to the bulgur. Cover and let stand for about 15 minutes.

5 In a serving bowl, combine the tomatoes, parsley, mint, and scallions. Add the bulgur and any dressing in the bowl and gently toss. Cover and refrigerate until ready to serve.

Bulgur

Bulgur—wheat berries that have been parboiled, dried, and ground—is popular throughout the Middle East. Because it is already partially cooked, it is a relatively fast-cooking grain. To prepare bulgur, either soak it in boiling water until it's soft and fluffy, usually about 20 minutes, or cook it on top of the stove in boiling water, about 10 minutes. This timing is for the tan-colored medium or coarse bulgur, which is the color and grain size I prefer. The bulgur from Bob's Red Mill is reddish brown and needs a longer soaking time than the cream-colored variety. If using this bulgur, you will need to double the soaking time in step 1 of the recipe on page 169; the texture and flavor will be excellent.

Toasted Pita, Tomato, and Feta Salad

I make *fatoosh*, or a pita and tomato salad, often, borrowing freely from many inspirations and my own culinary instincts. In the traditional recipe, day-old pita is moistened with water. But I prefer to enhance the crunch of the pita by first toasting it until it's crisp and golden. Then I spread the toasted pita on a deep platter and build the salad—a mélange of salad greens, ripe tomato, and cucumber—on top, so that the juice from the tomatoes and the dressing moisten the toasted pita just enough. **MAKES 4 SERVINGS**

2 whole-wheat pita breads

⅓ cup extra-virgin olive oil, plus more as needed for the pitas

½ teaspoon coarse salt, plus more as needed for the pitas

¼ cup fresh lemon juice

1 garlic clove, grated

2 teaspoons dried sumac (see page 27)

1 or 2 romaine lettuce hearts, cores removed, leaves cut crosswise into ½-inch slices (about 2 cups)

2 medium tomatoes, cored and cut into ½-inch chunks (about 2½ cups)

1 cup lightly packed coarsely chopped fresh flat-leaf (Italian) parsley leaves

1 cup lightly packed coarsely chopped fresh mint leaves

2 small cucumbers or ½ large seedless cucumber, peeled and cut into thin rounds (about 1 cup)

½ cup thinly sliced scallion (white and green parts), cut on the diagonal

1 cup crumbled feta (see page 62)

½ cup halved pitted kalamata olives

1 Preheat the oven to 350°F. Separate the pitas along the folded edges to make 4 rounds. Brush one side of each round with oil and sprinkle lightly with salt. Stack the rounds and, with a large knife, cut the stack into 8 wedges. Spread the pita wedges on two large baking sheets and bake until crisp and golden, 15 to 20 minutes. Let cool.

2 Meanwhile, whisk together the ⅓ cup oil, lemon juice, garlic, sumac, and ½ teaspoon salt in a small bowl.

3 Combine the lettuce, tomatoes, parsley, mint, cucumbers, and scallions in a large bowl. Add the dressing and toss.

4 Spread a layer of the toasted pita on a platter or on each of 4 dinner plates. Spoon the salad and any dressing left in the bowl over the pita. Crumble the feta on top and top with the olives.

Indonesian Vegetable Salad with Peanut Dressing

An Indonesian dish known as gado-gado, this is a beautifully composed salad consisting of both raw and cooked vegetables, hard-cooked eggs, and, in the variation that follows, squares of fried tofu, dressed with a subtly spiced creamy coconut and peanut sauce. A good way to serve this dish is to spread a portion of the dressing on the bottom of a large platter and then arrange the vegetables and other ingredients in mounds on top, alternating shapes and colors as you go. Then, once the platter is brought to the table for all to admire, toss the ingredients with the dressing on the bottom and serve. Pass bowls of cilantro and extra dressing to add as desired.

MAKES 4 TO 6 SERVINGS

1½ cups coconut milk

1 cup peanut butter (creamy or chunky)

3 tablespoons tamari or soy sauce (see page 44)

2 tablespoons fresh lime juice, plus more to taste

1 tablespoon tamarind paste, plus more to taste

1 tablespoon honey

1 tablespoon red curry paste, plus more to taste

2 teaspoons grated garlic

2 teaspoons grated peeled fresh ginger

1 teaspoon minced jalapeño pepper, plus more to taste

1 teaspoon coarse salt

3 or 4 smallish (about 12 ounces total) Yukon gold potatoes

1 large or 2 medium carrots, peeled and cut into 2-x-¼-inch sticks

4 ounces (about 1½ cups) snow peas, trimmed

2 baby bok choy, trimmed, cut crosswise into ½-inch slices

2 cups thinly sliced cabbage

2 cups bean sprouts, rinsed and drained

1 cup sliced (¼-inch pieces) seedless cucumber

1 cup sliced (⅛-inch pieces) radish

½ cup sliced scallion (white and green parts), cut on the diagonal

½ cup fresh cilantro leaves

½ cup coarsely chopped salted roasted peanuts

2 to 4 hard-cooked eggs, peeled and halved

1 Combine the coconut milk, peanut butter, tamari, lime juice, tamarind, honey, curry paste, garlic, ginger, jalapeño, and salt in a blender and blend until smooth. (If using chunky peanut butter, the dressing does not have to be smooth.) Taste and adjust the seasonings, adding more curry paste or jalapeño if you prefer more heat, or more tamarind or lime juice if you prefer more acid.

2 Place the potatoes in a medium saucepan, add water to cover, and bring to a boil. Cook, covered, until the potatoes are tender, about 20 minutes, depending on their size. Lift the potatoes from the water and set aside to cool. Add the carrot sticks to the simmering potato water. Cook, uncovered, until crisp-tender, about 3 minutes. Transfer to a bowl of cold water and then drain. Add the snow peas to the simmering water and cook, uncovered, until crisp-tender, about 2 minutes. Drain and rinse with cold water.

3 When the potatoes are cool enough to handle, use a paring knife to pull off the skins. Cut the potatoes into ¼-inch pieces and set aside.

4 When ready to serve, spread about half the dressing on a large platter. Reserve the remaining dressing to serve on the side. Make individual mounds of the cooked potatoes, carrots, and snow peas, and the bok choy, cabbage, bean sprouts, cucumber, and radishes. Sprinkle the scallions, cilantro, and peanuts on top. Tuck the halved hard-cooked eggs between the mounds of vegetables. Serve the remaining dressing on the side.

Variation

INDONESIAN VEGETABLE AND FRIED TOFU SALAD WITH PEANUT DRESSING

Marinated Tofu

- 12 ounces firm tofu
- 2 tablespoons tamari or soy sauce (see page 44)
- 2 tablespoons unseasoned Japanese rice vinegar
- 1 tablespoon honey
- 2 teaspoons Sriracha, or other hot chile paste

  Vegetable oil, for frying
- 2 tablespoons cornstarch, or as needed

1 Make the marinated tofu: Stand the tofu on end and cut into two thick, evenly sized slabs. Place a kitchen towel on a work surface, place the tofu on the towel, and fold the towel over the tofu. Place a small cutting board on top of the towel to press the excess moisture from the tofu. Let stand for about 20 minutes. By releasing the moisture, the tofu will absorb more of the marinade. Cut the tofu into $3/4$-inch squares and arrange in a single layer on a plate or tray.

2 In a small bowl, whisk together the tamari, vinegar, honey, and Sriracha until blended to make a marinade. Spoon evenly over the tofu. Cover and refrigerate for at least 30 minutes, or up to several hours, turning once.

3 Heat a wok or large heavy skillet over high heat until hot enough to sizzle a drop of water. Add ¼ inch of oil. When hot enough to sizzle the tofu, strain the tofu in a sieve to remove excess marinade. Spread the cornstarch in a small bowl or dish. Coat one piece of tofu at a time lightly with the cornstarch. Fry the tofu, gently turning with a small spatula as the pieces brown, about 2 to 3 minutes per side. Set aside on a dish as the tofu browns.

4 Follow the recipe for Indonesian Vegetable Salad with Peanut Dressing (beginning on page 172), adding the tofu to the platter with the other ingredients in step 4.

Potato Causa with Egg Salad and Avocado

Mashed potatoes typically layered with hard-cooked eggs and seafood and served cold is a classic preparation in Peruvian cuisine. In this recipe, the mashed potatoes are mixed with a bright yellow pepper paste called aji amarillo. You may be able to source it through a Latin grocer; it adds a brilliant yellow color to the potatoes, along with a pleasant, peppery tang. My vegetarian adaptation of the dish features layers of egg salad and mashed avocado flavored with lime and cilantro. **MAKES 4 SERVINGS**

Potato Layer

2 pounds potatoes, preferably Yukon gold

½ to 1 cup mayonnaise, as needed

4 to 6 tablespoons aji amarillo paste (see page 178), to taste

1 to 2 tablespoons fresh lime juice, plus more to taste

1 teaspoon coarse salt, plus more to taste

Egg Salad Layer

6 large eggs, hard-cooked and peeled

¼ cup mayonnaise

1 tablespoon finely chopped fresh parsley

1 tablespoon grated white onion

1 tablespoon fresh lime juice

Coarse salt and freshly ground black pepper

Avocado Layer

2 ripe avocados, halved, pitted, and peeled

1 tablespoon lime juice

1 tablespoon finely chopped fresh cilantro, plus 2 tablespoons coarsely chopped fresh cilantro leaves for garnish

Pinch of coarse salt

1 or 2 plum tomatoes, cut into 12 thin rounds, for garnish

1 Make the potato layer: Cook the potatoes in salted boiling water until tender when pierced with the tip of a knife, 20 to 25 minutes. Drain and let cool. Carefully peel the skins and cut the potatoes into chunks. Push the potatoes through a food mill or mash them with a potato masher. A food mill makes the potatoes smoother and is less labor-intensive. Do not use the food processor, because it will make the potatoes pasty.

2 Add ½ cup of the mayonnaise, aji amarillo paste, lime juice, and salt and stir with a wooden spoon until well blended. If the

mixture is too stiff, add more mayonnaise, 2 tablespoons at a time. Taste and add more lime juice and salt, if needed. Cover the potatoes and set aside.

3 Make the egg salad layer: Place the eggs in a bowl and coarsely chop with a pastry blender or break up with a fork. Add the mayonnaise, parsley, onion, lime juice, salt to taste, and a grinding of pepper and stir until thoroughly blended. Cover and set aside.

4 Make the avocado layer: Place the avocado in a bowl and mash with a fork. Add the lime juice, the finely chopped cilantro, and a pinch of salt; stir until well blended.

5 To assemble: Lightly brush the bottom and sides of an 8-inch baking dish (either glass or aluminum) with a thin film of oil. Using a rubber spatula or an offset spatula, spread one third of the potatoes in a smooth layer to the edges of the pan. Spoon the egg salad on top of the potato and spread in a smooth layer. Top with another one third of the potato mixture and gently spread in a smooth layer. Spoon the avocado on top and spread in an even layer to the edges. Top with the remaining potatoes and spread into a smooth, even layer.

6 Place the tomato slices on the top, clustering them into 4 rosettes so each serving will have a tomato cluster in the center.

7 Cover the pan and refrigerate until very cold, at least 4 hours or overnight. To serve, cut into squares and remove from the pan with a wide pancake turner.

Aji Amarillo

Aji amarillo (*aji* means chile pepper and *amarillo* means yellow in Spanish) is made from aji amarillo chiles, which can be quite hot. If the paste is not available, you can substitute Tabasco or Sriracha or another complex hot pepper sauce or paste. But taste as you add, as these will be much hotter, plus you won't get the wonderful bright golden color the aji amarillo brings to the potatoes. Look for aji amarillo, imported from Peru, in Latin food stores.

Tomato and Bread Salad

Known in Tuscany as panzanella, this bread and tomato salad is an Italian classic. The bread must be a coarse-grained chewy loaf, preferably from a local artisan bakery. (Other breads will turn mushy when wet with the tomato juices.) If you are lucky enough to know a baker who makes a rustic loaf studded with green or black olives, use it here. A rustic whole-grain loaf is another good option. **MAKES 4 SERVINGS**

4 to 6 thick (1-inch) slices from a rustic loaf of bread, preferably an olive bread or whole-grain loaf

Extra-virgin olive oil

1 garlic clove

¼ to ½ cup ice water

4 or 5 large juicy tomatoes (1½ to 2 pounds), stems trimmed

1 cup diced (¼-inch pieces) red onion

1 cup lightly packed torn fresh basil leaves

Coarse salt and freshly ground black pepper

2 tablespoons aged red wine vinegar

1 Preheat the oven to 350°F. Arrange the bread in a single layer on a large baking sheet. Brush both sides of the bread lightly with olive oil. Bake, flipping halfway through, until the bread is browned on both sides, about 10 minutes per side. Let cool. Cut into approximately 1-inch squares.

2 Bruise the garlic by pressing down on it with the side of a large knife. Rub the garlic all over the surface of a large salad bowl. Leave the remains of the garlic in the bowl. Add the bread cubes. Add a few tablespoons of the water at a time, tossing the bread after each addition. If the tomatoes are especially juicy, you may only need half of the water.

3 Cut the tomatoes into ½-inch cubes. Add to the bread along with the onion, basil, a generous sprinkling of salt, and a grinding of pepper. Drizzle about 3 tablespoons oil over the mixture and toss to blend. Sprinkle with the vinegar. Taste and season with more salt, olive oil, and/or vinegar, if needed.

Butternut Squash Korma,
page 224

MAIN DISHES

RICE AND GRAINS

Basmati Rice with Caramelized Yellow Onions **233**

Summer Garden Paella **236**

Evan's Jamaican Rice and Peas **239**

Kimchi Fried Rice **241**

Coconut Milk Rice Pilaf with Cilantro Sauce **243**

Farrotto with Broccolini and Parmigiano-Reggiano **244**

Mushroom Chilaquiles **246**

Baked Tortilla Casserole **250**

Bulgur Pilaf with Dried Apricots **251**

NOODLES AND PASTA

Thai Curried Rice Noodles with Dried Shiitake Mushrooms and Spinach **253**

Crisp Noodle Pancake with Stir-Fried Vegetables **255**

Cold Chinese Noodles with Peanut Sauce **258**

Pasta Gratin with Ricotta, Escarole, Acorn Squash, and Two Cheeses **260**

Noodles with Yogurt and Mint Sauce **263**

Summer Squash Pastitsio **264**

Chickpeas and Pasta with Artichoke Hearts **266**

Toasted Israeli Couscous with Sautéed Mushrooms, Cauliflower, and Peas **268**

BEANS

Egyptian Beans

Naguib Mahfouz, the Nobel prize–winning Egyptian author, wrote with reverence, in *The Cairo Trilogy*, of his mother's daily preparation of *ful*, the bean dish eaten for breakfast each morning. The visual of Mahfouz's descriptive prose has stayed with me over the years. *Ful*, or beans, are most typically dried fava beans. I am fortunate that my local market has an excellent section of imported products from the Middle East, with dried favas sold in 12-ounce bags. The ones I like are called yellow split beans (see Sources, page 308, for ordering information). **MAKES 4 SERVINGS**

12 ounces dried, split, and peeled fava beans

2 garlic cloves, bruised with the side of a knife

1 small wedge or slice onion

1 bay leaf

1 leafy celery top

1 small dried hot red chile pepper

¼ cup extra-virgin olive oil

Coarse salt

1 lemon, cut into wedges

½ teaspoon ground toasted cumin (see page 57, Step 1)

¼ cup finely chopped fresh flat-leaf (Italian) parsley

Warmed pita bread, for serving

1 Place the beans in a bowl and cover with water. Swish the water around and skim off any debris or bits of shell. Let the beans soak for 4 hours or overnight. Drain and place in a large saucepan. Add enough water to cover by about 2 inches and the garlic, onion, bay leaf, celery top, and chile. Bring to a boil. Reduce the heat and simmer, covered, adding small amounts of water, if necessary, to keep the beans covered with water, until very tender, 1 to 1½ hours or longer if necessary.

2 Ladle out about ½ cup of the cooking water and reserve. Drain the beans. Remove and discard the onion, bay leaf, celery top, and chile pepper.

3 In a large, shallow serving bowl, mash ½ cup of the cooked beans with the reserved ½ cup cooking water. Add the rest of the beans, the oil, and salt to taste and stir to blend. Arrange the lemon wedges around the edges of the bowl, sprinkle with the cumin and parsley, and serve with the pita bread.

Black Bean, Butternut Squash, and Mushroom Enchiladas with Poblano-Tomato Sauce

Enchiladas—here with a fragrant filling of soft cooked winter squash, black beans, and mushrooms—are a delicious make-ahead meal. I use two cheeses to melt all over the top. For a deep chile taste and a bit of heat, I add roasted poblano chile to both the filling and the sauce, as well as chipotle in adobo sauce and mild ground chile powder. **MAKES 6 SERVINGS**

Enchiladas

- 1 large poblano chile
- 1 pound butternut squash, cut into 2-inch chunks
- 2 tablespoons extra-virgin olive oil, or more as needed
- ½ cup finely chopped onion
- 8 ounces cremini mushrooms, coarsely chopped (about 3 cups)
- Coarse salt
- ½ teaspoon ground cumin
- ½ teaspoon chile powder
- ½ teaspoon Mexican oregano (see page 110)
- 1 can (14.5 ounces) black beans, rinsed and drained
- 1½ cups (about 8 ounces) Requesón cheese or ricotta (see page 186)
- 12 (6-inch) corn tortillas

Sauce

- 1 tablespoon extra-virgin olive oil
- 1 garlic clove, grated
- 1 teaspoon ground cumin
- 1 teaspoon chile powder

- 3½ cups canned crushed tomatoes or pureed whole tomatoes
- 1 teaspoon coarse salt, plus more to taste
- 1 to 2 teaspoons finely chopped chipotle in adobo sauce (see page 130), or to taste
- ½ teaspoon Mexican oregano (see page 110)
- ¼ cup chopped fresh cilantro
- 1½ cups coarsely shredded queso Chihuahua (see page 249), Monterey Jack, or mozzarella cheese
- 1½ to 2 cups crema (see page 249) or stirred sour cream

1 Make the enchiladas: Preheat the broiler, with the shelf 2 to 3 inches from the heat source. Line a baking sheet with foil and place the poblano on the foil. Broil, turning the pepper as it blisters and chars, about 5 minutes per side. Remove from the broiler and wrap the poblano in the foil. Once cool, unwrap and rub off the charred skin. Split the poblano lengthwise in half. Remove and discard the stem and seeds and finely chop the flesh. You should have about ½ cup. Set aside. *continued >*

2 Place the squash in a steamer basket and steam, covered, until the flesh is fork-tender, 15 to 20 minutes. Remove from the heat and let cool. When cool enough to handle, cut off the skin and cut the flesh into ½-inch pieces. Set aside.

3 Heat the oil in a large skillet over medium heat. Add the onion and cook, stirring, until golden, about 5 minutes. Add the mushrooms and sprinkle lightly with salt. Cook, stirring, until well browned, about 10 minutes, adding drizzles of olive oil, if needed. Add the cumin, chile powder, and oregano. Add the reserved squash, the black beans, and about ¼ cup of the poblano. Cook over medium-low heat, stirring, until heated through. Remove from the heat, crumble the Requesón on top, and let stand until ready to use.

4 Preheat the oven to 300°F. Wrap the tortillas in foil and place in the oven to soften.

5 Make the sauce: In a deep skillet, combine the oil and garlic over medium-low heat and heat, stirring, until the garlic begins to sizzle. Add the cumin and chile powder and cook, stirring, for about 10 seconds. Add the remaining reserved poblano, tomatoes, salt, chipotles, and oregano. Bring to a boil, reduce the heat, and simmer, uncovered, until the sauce is slightly thickened, about

15 minutes. Stir in the cilantro. Taste and add more salt or chipotle, if needed.

6 Ladle about half of the sauce into a 13-x-9-inch baking dish. Remove the tortillas from the oven and increase the temperature to 350°F.

7 Lay the tortillas on a work surface and spoon the filling, dividing evenly, down the center of each. Roll each tortilla loosely over the filling and place, snugly, seam side down, on the sauce in the baking dish. Spread the remaining sauce on top. Sprinkle with the shredded cheese. Cover loosely with foil and bake until the cheese is melted and the enchiladas are hot, about 25 minutes, if the enchiladas are at room temperature. The enchiladas can be assembled 1 to 2 days ahead, refrigerated, and baked until the cheese is melted and enchiladas are hot, 45 to 50 minutes before serving.

8 Before serving, drizzle some crema over the top, and serve a bowl of it on the side.

Requesón

Requesón (Mexican ricotta) can be quite dry and crumbly. If using Italian ricotta, spoon it into a strainer and let stand for at least 1 hour to remove excess moisture.

Fava Beans and Greens, Pugliese Style

Called *fave e cicoria*, or fava beans and chicory, this is a specialty of Puglia, a relatively undiscovered region of Italy situated along the southeast portion of the boot. The fava bean, native to North Africa, is tan and shaped like a lima bean but with a bumpy texture. Some whole dried favas—like fresh favas—require peeling after cooking, which takes time. Fortunately, they do come dried, split, and peeled (sometimes labeled dried yellow split beans), which I highly recommend. Look for dried fava beans in Italian or Middle Eastern grocers, and make sure they say yellow split beans on the package. The others are big and brown and when cooked, although soft on the inside, are leathery and tough on the outside. Canned favas (found in Middle Eastern groceries) are not an option. Fava Beans and Greens are delicious eaten with slivers of cheese from the region: either a piccante provolone or a caciocavallo. Both cheeses are available wherever imported Italian cheeses are sold. MAKES 4 SERVINGS

12 ounces dried, split, and peeled yellow fava beans

1 potato (6 ounces), peeled and cubed

4 garlic cloves, thinly sliced

1 sprig fresh flat-leaf (Italian) parsley

¼ cup extra-virgin olive oil, plus more for greens and for serving

2 tablespoons fresh lemon juice or water

1½ teaspoons coarse salt, plus more for greens and to taste

1 pound chicory, dandelion, broccoli rabe, or other bitter greens, rinsed, tips of stems trimmed, and cut into 2-inch lengths

Italian bread, for serving

Shaved imported provolone or caciocavallo, for serving (optional)

1 Place the beans in a bowl and add water to cover. Use a slotted spoon to remove any bits of bean that float to the top. Drain the beans and place in a large, wide pot. Add about 6 cups water, or enough to cover the beans by about ½ inch.

2 Add the potato, garlic, and parsley to the water and bring to a boil. Cook over low heat, partially covered, stirring often and adding a splash of water from time to time, if necessary, to keep the beans covered with water. Cook until the beans are soft and bordering on mushy, anywhere from 45 minutes to 1 hour and 15 minutes, depending on the dryness of the bean. Once they are soft, remove from the heat, uncover, and let cool slightly. If the beans seem soupy, they'll

absorb the excess moisture as they cool. If they are very stiff, you might want to add an extra splash of water.

3 Discard the parsley sprig if it hasn't cooked away. (The garlic and potato will have practically dissolved by now.) Stir in the oil, lemon juice, and salt. Transfer the mixture to a food mill set over a bowl and puree. Return the mixture to the pot. Taste and add more salt and olive oil, if needed. Just before serving, reheat, stirring, over low heat until warmed.

4 Meanwhile, bring a large pot two thirds filled with water to a boil. Add 1 tablespoon of salt. Add the greens and boil gently until very tender, 6 to 8 minutes for dandelions, chicory, or broccoli rabe. (Italians never serve their greens toothsome, but you can cook them to the texture you desire.) Drain the greens and return to the pot. Drizzle with a stream of olive oil and sprinkle with a pinch of salt and toss to coat. Keep warm. (Some cooks like to add a pinch of crushed red pepper, but it's not typical.)

5 To serve, spread the beans on a platter, making ridges in the puree (to hold the olive oil). Mound the greens in the center of the puree. Drizzle with olive oil. Serve with thick slices of grilled or toasted Italian bread and the cheese, if desired.

Eggplant Balls in Pomegranate Tomato Sauce

In the Eastern Mediterranean, where eggplant reigns, eggplant "meat" balls are ubiquitous from Turkey to Morocco, where they're called *kefta*, and north to Sicily and up the Italian boot, where they are called *polpette*. This recipe represents a composite of these popular recipes. The eggplants are roasted until soft and then combined with sautéed onion and garlic, coarse dry bread crumbs, egg, feta, chickpeas, and herbs. The resulting balls are super tender and the flavors perfectly blended. The recipe is from my friend, Brooke Jackson. **MAKES 20 TO 24, ENOUGH FOR 4 SERVINGS**

1 large eggplant (about 1 pound), trimmed and halved lengthwise

2 tablespoons extra-virgin olive oil, plus an optional 2 tablespoons for the sauce

1 tablespoon chopped fresh parsley

1 tablespoon chopped fresh mint

1 tablespoon chopped fresh dill

¼ cup chopped onion

1 garlic clove, grated

½ teaspoon ground cumin

½ cup cooked dried or rinsed and drained canned chickpeas

2 tablespoons crumbled feta cheese (see page 62)

1 large egg

1 teaspoon coarse salt, plus more to taste

½ teaspoon freshly ground black pepper, plus more to taste

½ cup coarse dry bread crumbs or panko, or more as needed

⅔ cup fine dry bread crumbs, for breading

Vegetable oil, for frying

3½ cups Roasted Plum Tomatoes (page 103) or canned chopped tomatoes with their juices

1 tablespoon pomegranate molasses (see page 26)

1 Preheat the oven to 400°F. Make several ½-inch-deep slits in the cut surface of the eggplants. Use 1 tablespoon of the olive oil to lightly coat the cut side of the eggplants and place, cut side up, on a baking sheet. Bake until golden and tender, 40 to 45 minutes. Let cool.

2 Finely chop the parsley, mint, and dill together. Measure out 1½ tablespoons and reserve separately.

3 Heat the remaining 1 tablespoon of olive oil in a small skillet until hot enough to sizzle a piece of onion. Add the onion and cook over medium-low heat, stirring, until golden, about 5 minutes. Stir in the garlic and cumin and remove from the heat.

4 Scoop the flesh from the eggplant and transfer to the bowl of a food processor. You should have about 1½ cups. Add the onion mixture, chickpeas, feta, egg, 1½ tablespoons reserved herbs, salt, and pepper and pulse just until coarsely chopped. Do not puree. Transfer to a bowl. Stir in the coarse bread crumbs to make a thick mixture that will easily shape into balls.

5 Using about 1 rounded tablespoon for each ball, shape with lightly dampened hands into 20 to 24 small balls and line up on a tray. Refrigerate the balls for 30 minutes.

6 Spread the fine dry bread crumbs on a large plate and roll each ball in the crumbs to lightly coat. Meanwhile, heat about ½ inch of vegetable oil in a large, deep skillet until hot enough to sizzle a pinch of bread crumbs. Have ready a tray or baking sheet lined with a double layer of paper towels. Add the balls, about 6 at a time, to the hot oil and fry, turning gently with the tip of a spoon as they brown, until evenly

dark golden brown, about 5 minutes total cooking time. (Tongs may crush the tender balls.) Remove from the oil with a slotted spoon and drain on the paper towels. Repeat with the remaining eggplant balls. The eggplant balls can be made 1 to 2 days ahead and refrigerated.

7 Puree the tomatoes in a blender or food processor. The sauce should be smooth. In a large skillet, combine the pureed tomatoes with 2 tablespoons olive oil if using canned tomatoes. Add the pomegranate molasses. Bring to a boil, reduce the heat, and simmer, uncovered, until the sauce is thickened and the oil has separated from the tomatoes, about 20 minutes. Stir in the remaining herbs (you should have about 1½ tablespoons) and add salt and pepper to taste.

8 Preheat the oven to 350°F. Arrange the eggplant balls in a shallow oven-to-table casserole dish. Spoon the sauce over the top, cover, and reheat in the oven, about 15 minutes if the balls were at room temperature. If the eggplant balls and sauce were made ahead and refrigerated, reheat for about 25 minutes.

Lentils, Rice, and Macaroni with Spicy Tomato Sauce

In Egypt, this fortifying, much-loved street food is dished out in rhythmic precision from one pot of lentils, one of rice, and one of pasta. The mix is topped with a spicy tomato sauce. Crisp-fried shallots and/or chickpeas are optional toppings. A spice blend called baharat adds a distinctive taste to the tomato sauce. It is available in some Middle Eastern grocers, but you can easily make it by approximating the spices. The overall recipe can be quite labor-intensive, but I often prepare a few of the components—the spice blend, the tomato sauce, and the fried onions or fried chickpeas—a day or two ahead. **MAKES 6 TO 8 SERVINGS**

¼ cup plus 2 tablespoons extra-virgin olive oil

¼ cup finely chopped onion

1 garlic clove, grated, plus 1 teaspoon grated garlic for the garlic oil

3 teaspoons Baharat (recipe follows), or more to taste

1 can (28 ounces) crushed tomatoes with their juices

3½ teaspoons coarse salt

5½ cups water

1 cup brown lentils

1 cup basmati rice

½ cup small macaroni (elbow or bucatini)

Crisp-Fried Shallots or Onions (page 203) and/or Crisp-Fried Chickpeas (recipe follows), for serving (optional)

1 Heat 2 tablespoons of the oil in a large, deep skillet until hot enough to sizzle the onion. Add the onion and cook over medium-low heat, stirring, until the onion begins to brown, about 5 minutes. Stir in the garlic clove and 2 teaspoons of the Baharat and cook, stirring, for about 30 seconds. Add the tomatoes and ½ teaspoon of the salt. Rinse out the tomato can with about ½ cup water and add it to the sauce; bring to a boil. Reduce the heat to maintain a gentle simmer and cook until the sauce is thickened, about 20 minutes. Keep warm until ready to serve.

2 In a large, broad pan, bring the remaining 5 cups water to a boil. Add the lentils and cook, covered, over medium-low heat for about 20 minutes. Stir in the rice and 2 teaspoons salt and cook, covered, until the rice and lentils are both tender and the water is absorbed, about 20 minutes more. (If the water is not fully absorbed, drain in a colander or large strainer.) Place the lentils and rice in a large heatproof serving

bowl and cover with foil to keep warm until ready to serve. (They can also be kept warm in an oven set at its lowest temperature, about 250°F.)

3 Meanwhile, bring a small saucepan three quarters filled with water to a boil. Add the macaroni and the remaining 1 teaspoon salt and boil, uncovered, until the macaroni is tender, about 12 minutes. Drain and add to the bowl with the lentils and rice; stir to combine.

4 In a small skillet, combine the remaining ¼ cup oil, the remaining 1 teaspoon grated garlic, and the remaining 1 teaspoon Baharat and heat, stirring, until the oil is hot enough to sizzle the garlic, about 1 minute. Pour over the lentil mixture and toss to coat.

5 Reheat the tomato sauce, if necessary. To serve, spoon the lentil mixture into bowls, top with the tomato sauce, and sprinkle with the Crisp-Fried Shallots or Onions and/ or the Crisp-Fried Chickpeas, if using.

Baharat (Egyptian Spice Blend)

MAKES ABOUT ¼ CUP

- 2 teaspoons whole black peppercorns
- 2 teaspoons cumin seeds
- 1 teaspoon coriander seeds
- ½ teaspoon crushed red pepper flakes, or more if you like
- 6 whole cloves
- 2 teaspoons sweet paprika
- ½ teaspoon ground cinnamon

Combine the peppercorns, cumin, coriander, red pepper flakes, and cloves in a small, heavy skillet. Heat the spices over medium-low heat, stirring, until lightly toasted and fragrant, about 3 minutes. Stir the paprika and cinnamon into the hot mixture. Transfer to a saucer and let stand until cool. Transfer to a spice grinder and grind into a fine powder, or use a mortar and pestle or a peppermill. Store the spice mixture in an airtight tin or glass jar.

Crisp-Fried Chickpeas

These make a great snack or garnish for salad, grain dishes, or vegetable stews. To get the best results, the chickpeas need to be air-dried for several hours or overnight.

MAKES ABOUT 2 CUPS

1½ to 2 cups canned or cooked dried chickpeas

Vegetable oil, for frying

Coarse salt, smoked paprika, garlic powder, curry powder, or chile powder (optional)

1 Drain the chickpeas and spread on a tray lined with a kitchen towel. Allow the chickpeas to air-dry for at least 6 hours or overnight. Do not cover.

2 In a deep skillet, heat ¼ inch of oil until hot enough to sizzle one chickpea. With a slotted spoon, gradually add the chickpeas. Fry, adjusting the heat as necessary to maintain a steady sizzle, stirring, until the chickpeas are golden brown, about 10 minutes.

3 Lift the chickpeas from the hot oil with a slotted spoon and place them in a strainer set over a bowl. Shake the chickpeas for a few seconds to get rid of the excess oil. Sprinkle the hot chickpeas lightly with salt or any of the other suggested seasonings while they are still in the strainer.

Chickpea and Mushroom Moussaka

In this spin on moussaka, eggplant is layered with cheese and a chunky tomato, chickpea, and mushroom sauce fragrant with cinnamon and fresh chopped dill, mint, and parsley. You can roast the eggplant slices, make the tomato sauce, and/or make the cream sauce a day or two ahead, and assemble the casserole just before baking and serving. The casserole can also be completely put together a day or several hours ahead and refrigerated, covered, until ready to bake. MAKES 6 TO 8 SERVINGS

Roasted Eggplant

- 3 medium eggplants (about 2 pounds), trimmed and cut into ¼-inch-thick slices

  Coarse salt, as needed

  Extra-virgin olive oil, as needed

Mushroom and Chickpea Sauce

- ¼ cup extra-virgin olive oil, plus more as needed

- 1 cup chopped onion

- 1 can (14.5 ounces) chickpeas, well drained, or 1½ cups cooked dried chickpeas

- 12 ounces cremini mushrooms (or a combination of different varieties), coarsely chopped (4 to 5 cups)

  Coarse salt

  Freshly ground black pepper

- 2 garlic cloves, finely chopped

- 2 tablespoons chopped fresh mint

- 2 tablespoons chopped fresh dill

- 2 tablespoons chopped fresh flat-leaf (Italian) parsley

- 1 can (28 ounces) crushed tomatoes with their juices or 3 cups Roasted Plum Tomatoes (page 103), pureed

- 1 teaspoon ground cinnamon

- ½ to 1 cup water, if needed

Béchamel Sauce

- 2 tablespoons extra-virgin olive oil

- 2 tablespoons all-purpose flour

- 2 cups whole milk or half-and-half

- ½ cup grated Parmigiano-Reggiano

- 1 teaspoon ground cinnamon

- ½ teaspoon coarse salt

  Freshly ground black pepper

Assembly

- 4 tablespoons fine dry bread crumbs

- 1 cup shredded mozzarella cheese, plus additional thin slices mozzarella (about 2 ounces) for topping

....

1 Make the eggplant: Layer the eggplant slices in a colander, sprinkling each layer lightly with salt. Set the colander over a large bowl, place a plate on top of the eggplant, and weight it with something heavy, such as a small iron skillet or a large can of tomatoes. Let stand for at least 1 hour. Place the colander in the sink and rinse off the salt. Lay the eggplant slices on a large kitchen towel and blot dry.

2 Meanwhile, preheat the oven to 400°F. Line two or three baking sheets with parchment paper and arrange the eggplant in single layers on each. Brush the tops lightly with oil. Roast until lightly browned and tender, 20 to 25 minutes, changing the positions of the pans halfway through the cooking time. Let cool. If you are making the moussaka right away, reduce the oven temperature to 350°F.

3 Make the Mushroom and Chickpea Sauce: In a deep skillet, heat the oil until hot enough to sizzle a piece of onion. Add the onion and cook over medium-low heat, stirring, until translucent and beginning to change color, about 8 minutes. Add the chickpeas and cook, stirring, for about 5 minutes. Add the mushrooms, a pinch of salt, and a grinding of pepper and cook over medium-high heat, stirring, until the mushroom juices are cooked down, about 5 minutes. Add the garlic, mint, dill, and parsley and cook, stirring, for about 1 minute. Add the tomatoes and cinnamon and bring to a boil. If the sauce is very thick, add ½ to 1 cup water. Reduce the heat to medium-low and simmer until the sauce is cooked down slightly, 15 to 20 minutes.

4 Make the Béchamel Sauce: Heat the oil in a medium saucepan until hot. Stir in the flour and cook over medium-low heat, stirring, until the flour bubbles and turns golden, about 3 minutes. Gradually whisk in the milk and cook, gently whisking, until the sauce is smooth and thick. Remove from the heat. Stir in the grated cheese, cinnamon, salt, and a grinding of pepper. The sauce will be thin, but will thicken as it cools, about 10 minutes. Set aside.

5 Assemble the moussaka: Preheat the oven to 350°F if necessary. Make an even layer of eggplant slices (about 8 to 10 per layer) in a shallow 2-quart baking dish. Sprinkle with 2 tablespoons of the bread crumbs and ⅓ cup of the shredded mozzarella. Top with half of the Mushroom and Chickpea Sauce. Arrange another layer of eggplant slices, sprinkle with the remaining 2 tablespoons bread crumbs and ⅓ cup more mozzarella, and spoon the remaining mushroom sauce on top. Arrange the remaining eggplant slices on top and sprinkle with the remaining ⅓ cup shredded mozzarella.

6 Pour the Béchamel Sauce evenly over the top. Arrange the slices of cheese on top. Bake until the top is bubbly and the edges golden, about 45 minutes. Cool for at least 15 minutes before cutting into squares and serving.

Roasted Butternut Squash and Black Bean Stew with Queso Fresco

This soulful black and orange stew gets a bit of heat from the poblano chiles and some sweetness from the roasted squash. The prevailing spice is cumin. For this stew I prefer the texture of cooked dried beans to canned. They can be soaked and cooked ahead and frozen for later use.

MAKES 4 TO 6 SERVINGS

1 poblano chile

1 large butternut squash (about 2 pounds)

4 tablespoons extra-virgin olive oil

1 teaspoon ground cumin

Coarse salt

1 cup chopped onion

2 garlic cloves, chopped

1 can (28 ounces) crushed tomatoes

2½ cups cooked dried black beans or 2 cans (14.5 ounces each) black beans, drained

1 cup (about 4 ounces) crumbled queso fresco (see page 249) or mild feta (see page 62)

2 tablespoons chopped fresh cilantro

1 Preheat the broiler. Line a baking sheet with foil and place the poblano on the foil. Broil, about 2 to 3 inches from the heat, turning the pepper as it blisters and chars, about 5 minutes per side. Remove and wrap in the foil. Once cool, unwrap and rub off the charred skin. Split the poblano in half. Remove and discard the stems and seeds and finely chop the flesh. You should have about ¼ cup. Set aside.

2 Preheat the oven to 400°F. Halve the squash or cut into large chunks. Use a small spoon to scoop out the seeds and membranes. Peel off the hard skin with a paring knife or vegetable peeler. Cut the squash into ½- to 1-inch chunks, pile them in the center of a baking sheet, drizzle with 2 tablespoons of the oil, and sprinkle with ½ teaspoon of the cumin and a sprinkling of salt. Toss to evenly coat and then spread the squash in a single layer. Roast until tender and lightly browned, about 40 minutes.

3 Meanwhile, heat the remaining 2 tablespoons oil in a shallow pan until hot enough to sizzle a piece of onion. Add the onion, garlic, and reserved poblano. Cook, stirring, over medium heat until the onion is softened and golden, about 8 minutes. Add the tomatoes, beans, roasted squash, and remaining ½ teaspoon cumin and heat, stirring gently, until simmering. Add salt to taste. Spread the cheese evenly on top, cover, and cook until the cheese is softened, about 10 minutes. Sprinkle with the cilantro before serving.

Cannellini Beans in Parmesan Tomato Broth

A cross between a soup and a stew, this dish is reminiscent of an extra-thick minestrone, but with fewer ingredients than traditional ones. It was inspired by a dish I remember my grandmother making. I save the rinds from wedges of Parmigiano-Reggiano to add to it and to other slow-cooked dishes such as polenta and risotto. The rinds—simply the dried outside edges—impart an extraordinary richness and texture as they soften and turn chewy. Cut them into small pieces and save in a plastic bag in the freezer where they'll be safe forever, it seems. If Parmigiano rinds aren't available, use grated cheese for plenty of flavor, albeit no texture. My first choice of bean for this dish is dried cannellini beans. The creamy texture cannot be matched by their canned counterparts. MAKES 4 SERVINGS

1 cup dried cannellini beans

3 tablespoons extra-virgin olive oil

1 cup thinly sliced onion

½ cup thinly sliced celery

½ cup thinly sliced peeled carrot

1 garlic clove, bruised with the side of a knife

4 cups water, plus more as needed

3 tablespoons tomato paste

⅓ cup chopped (¼-inch pieces) Parmigiano-Reggiano rinds or ½ cup grated Parmigiano-Reggiano, plus additional grated Parmigiano-Reggiano, for serving

1 dried chile pepper or pinch of crushed red pepper flakes, or to taste

¼ cup elbow macaroni or other small pasta shape

2 small zucchini, trimmed and diced into ½-inch cubes (about 1¾ cups)

2 tablespoons finely chopped fresh parsley or basil (in season)

Coarse salt

Freshly ground black pepper

1 Place the beans in a bowl or other container and cover with at least 2 inches of water. Let stand for at least 4 hours or as long as overnight. Add more water if needed to keep the beans covered. Drain before using.

2 Combine the oil, onion, celery, carrot, and garlic in a large, broad saucepan. Cook, stirring, over medium-low heat until the onion is a pale golden color, about 10 minutes. Add the water and the soaked and drained cannellini beans and bring to a boil. Reduce the heat and simmer the beans, partially

covered, until tender, 1 to 1½ hours, adding more water, ½ to 1 cup at a time, if the mixture gets too dry. (The mixture should be stewlike as compared to soupy.)

3 Stir in the tomato paste, Parmigiano rinds or grated cheese, and chile pepper (if using) and bring back to a boil. Lower the heat and simmer, covered, for about 30 minutes. Stir in the pasta and cook for 10 minutes. Add more water, ¼ cup at a time, if necessary, to keep the mixture thick but not dried out and sticking to the bottom of the pan. Stir in the zucchini and parsley and cook until both pasta and zucchini are tender, about 10 minutes more. Taste and add salt and a grinding of black pepper, if needed. Ladle into shallow bowls and serve sprinkled with additional cheese.

Dal

It is probably safe to say that for every cook in India there is a version of dal. The word can be confusing, given that it refers both to dried legumes and the finished dish, which can be either thin and soupy or thick and creamy. Most dal is made with yellow split peas. If you buy the peas in an Indian grocery store, the bag will say chana dal. I like to ladle this creamy, mildly spicy pureed version over rice and top it with Crisp-Fried Onions (page 203). **MAKES 4 SERVINGS**

1 cup yellow split peas

3 cups water, plus more as needed

1 large (about 8 ounces) ripe tomato, cored and cut into ½-inch wedges, or ⅔ cup canned plum tomatoes

½ cup chopped onion

1 garlic clove, chopped

1 teaspoon chopped peeled fresh ginger

1 small dried red chile or fresh serrano pepper, halved lengthwise (optional)

½ teaspoon ground turmeric

½ teaspoon coarse salt

2 tablespoons ghee (see page 76) or vegetable oil

½ teaspoon cumin seeds or black (brown) mustard seeds (see page 100)

Plain cooked rice, preferably basmati, for serving (optional)

Crisp-Fried Onions (page 203; optional)

¼ cup finely chopped fresh cilantro (optional)

1 Place the split peas in a bowl and add water to cover. Swirl the peas and skim and discard any debris that rises to the top. Drain and transfer to a medium saucepan.

2 Add the water, tomato, onion, garlic, ginger, dried red chile (if using), turmeric, and salt to the saucepan. Bring to a boil, stir once, and cook over medium-low heat, covered, until the peas are soft enough to crush easily with the back of a spoon on the side of the pan, 45 minutes to 1 hour. (Add more water, ½ cup at a time, if the dal becomes too thick or dry.) Let cool slightly.

3 Set a food mill over a large bowl and puree the peas. Return to the saucepan and keep warm.

4 Heat the ghee in a small skillet until hot enough to sizzle a couple of cumin seeds. Add the seeds and stir in the hot oil for about 10 seconds. Remove from the heat. Drizzle into the dal.

5 Ladle the dal into small bowls and eat as a soup or ladle it over hot cooked rice. Garnish with Crisp-Fried Onions or cilantro, if desired.

Crisp-Fried Onions or Shallots

I love these served on plain rice or other grains, vegetable pilaf, or soup such as dal. I learned to master Crisp-Fried Onions from Indian cooking teacher, cookbook author, and journalist Julie Sahni. To recrisp the onions if they go limp, spread the onions on a baking sheet and reheat them in a 350°F oven for about 10 minutes and they will crisp up very nicely.

MAKES ABOUT 1 CUP

1 or 2 small to medium onions, cut into thick wedges from top to root, or 1 pound shallots, peeled

Vegetable oil, for frying

1 To slice the onions paper-thin, use the serrated slicing blade of a food processor. Stack the wedges in the feed tube, end to end. With just a little pressure on the pusher, the onions will be sliced. Repeat until you have about 2 cups thinly sliced onion. Or, if preferred, cut the onions into thin, crescent-shaped slices by hand. If using shallots, slice in the food processor in the same manner or cut into paper-thin rounds with a sharp knife.

2 Have ready a strainer set over a bowl. Heat about ½ inch of oil in a medium heavy skillet until it ripples and quickly sizzles an onion slice. Add the onion slices, in batches, and cook over medium-high heat, stirring, until well browned, 15 to 20 minutes. With a skimmer, remove the onions from the oil to the strainer. Repeat with the remaining onions. (Do not drain the onions on paper towels, as the paper will make them soggy.) Let cool completely before transferring to an airtight container. They will keep, refrigerated, for 2 weeks or more. To recrisp, spread the onions on a baking sheet and heat them in a preheated 350°F oven for about 10 minutes. Reserve the onion-infused oil for future onion frying or to season other dishes.

Pumpkin and Black Bean Stew with Prunes and Apples

This black bean stew recipe is a cross between a Brazilian feijoada and a stew traditionally cooked in a pumpkin shell called *carbonada criolla*, without the beef. The main seasoning is oregano, which cooks down in the sofrito, or sauté of onion, bell pepper, and garlic, a mixture that is found in Spanish-influenced cuisine throughout the world. Some recipes for *carbonada criolla* call for fresh fruit; others use dried fruit. Being a fan of both I used one of each. Look for a squash with a relatively dry flesh, such as hubbard or kabocha. The cooking time of this all-vegetable stew is relatively short. It is great served with cornbread to soak up the delicious juices.

MAKES 4 SERVINGS

2 tablespoons extra-virgin olive oil

½ cup finely chopped onion

½ cup finely chopped green and/or red bell pepper

1 garlic clove, finely chopped

½ teaspoon crushed red pepper flakes, or more to taste

½ teaspoon dried oregano

1 can (14.5 ounces) whole or diced plum tomatoes with their juices or 1¾ cups Roasted Plum Tomatoes (page 103)

1¾ cups Roasted Vegetable Broth (page 120)

1¾ pounds pumpkin or other winter squash, peeled, seeded, and cut into ½-inch cubes (about 3 cups)

1 small (8 ounces) sweet potato, peeled and cut into ½-inch cubes (about 1 cup)

½ teaspoon coarse salt

1½ to 2 cups dried cooked or rinsed and drained canned black beans

1 cup corn kernels, fresh, canned, or thawed frozen

1 cup cubed (½-inch pieces) firm cooking apple, such as Granny Smith or Golden Delicious

½ cup (about 10) pitted prunes (dried plums)

6 ounces cotija cheese (see page 249) or other firm, salty cheese, such as Asiago, Grana Padano, or feta (see page 62), cut into ¼-inch cubes

¼ cup chopped fresh cilantro, including stems

1 Heat the oil in a large, deep skillet with a lid until hot enough to sizzle a piece of onion. Add the onion and bell pepper and cook over medium-low heat, stirring, until the onion is golden, about 10 minutes. Stir in the garlic, red pepper flakes, and oregano and cook for about 1 minute.

2 Stir in the tomatoes and bring to a boil. Boil, stirring, over medium-high heat until the tomatoes are reduced to a paste, about 10 minutes. Add the broth, pumpkin, sweet potato, and salt. Bring to a boil and cook over medium-low heat, covered, until the vegetables are tender, 15 to 20 minutes.

3 Add the beans, corn, apple, and prunes and cook, uncovered, stirring, until heated through and the apple is still crisp-tender, about 10 minutes. Top with the cubes of cheese and the chopped cilantro and serve in deep, wide soup bowls. As the cheese is stirred into the stew it will melt slightly and flavor the sauce.

VEGETABLES

Blini with Caramelized Cabbage, Honey Mustard, Sour Cream, and Dill

In St. Petersburg, from street kiosks to white-tablecloth restaurants, I learned all blini are not served with caviar. There I ate unleavened Russian-style crepes wrapped around a delicious filling of caramelized cabbage. If you like to make crepes, use your favorite recipe and go for it. If you're more into cooking in the fast lane, there are two alternatives: premade crepes (sometimes available in the produce section during strawberry season) or good-quality thin flour tortillas. The flour tortilla isn't authentic, but it sure is delicious warmed, smeared with honey mustard, filled with the cabbage and dill, sometimes rolled in crumbs, and sautéed in butter. **MAKES 6 SERVINGS**

5 tablespoons extra-virgin olive oil

10 cups coarsely chopped green cabbage (about 1½ pounds)

1 cup chopped onion

6 (8-inch) thin flour tortillas or crepes

1 tablespoon honey

2 teaspoons fresh lemon juice

1 teaspoon coarse salt, plus more to taste

Freshly ground black pepper

4 to 6 tablespoons honey mustard (store-bought)

¼ cup finely chopped fresh dill

½ cup fine dry bread crumbs (optional)

1 cup sour cream or plain Greek-style yogurt

1 Heat 3 tablespoons of the oil in a large, deep skillet over medium heat until hot enough to sizzle a piece of cabbage. Add the cabbage and onion, and cook, covered, for about 10 minutes. Uncover and cook over medium to medium-low heat, stirring, until the cabbage is reduced in volume by half and has turned a light golden color, 10 to 15 minutes more.

2 Meanwhile, preheat the oven to 300°F. Wrap the tortillas in foil and warm in the oven for about 10 minutes.

3 Add the honey, lemon juice, salt, and a grinding of pepper to the cabbage and stir to blend. Taste and add more salt if needed.

continued >

4 Spread about 1 tablespoon of the mustard on each warmed tortilla. Spoon the cabbage in the center, dividing evenly. Top each with a scant tablespoon of the dill. Fold the top and bottom sections of the tortilla so that the two opposite rounded sides slightly overlap on top of the cabbage, then fold in the left and right sides in the same manner. Turn, seam sides down; let stand until ready to cook.

5 Heat the remaining 2 tablespoons oil in a large skillet over medium-low heat. If using the bread crumbs, spread them on a plate, brush the surface of the blini lightly with some of the oil, and gently turn the filled blini in the bread crumbs until lightly coated. Place the blini seam sides down in the hot oil and cook until lightly browned, about 2 minutes. Turn with a wide spatula and lightly brown the other side, about 2 minutes more. Serve with the sour cream.

Zucchini "Lasagna"

A riff on the typical pasta-based lasagna, this recipe is pasta-free. The layers are made with lengthwise slices of roasted zucchini, two layers of tomato slices, panko crumbs, and lots of melting cheese in a rectangular baking dish. To make a meal in summer, serve with a fresh tomato, cucumber, and black olive salad and corn on the cob. **MAKES 4 SERVINGS**

Extra-virgin olive oil

2 pounds medium zucchini, trimmed and cut lengthwise into ⅛- to ¼-inch-thick slices

1 cup panko bread crumbs

½ cup lightly packed grated Parmigiano-Reggiano

2 teaspoons grated lemon zest

Coarse salt and freshly ground black pepper

2 large tomatoes, cored and cut into ¼-inch-thick slices

2 tablespoons thinly slivered fresh basil leaves

2 cups coarsely shredded or diced mozzarella cheese

1 Preheat the oven to 350°F. Brush a large baking sheet with a light coating of oil. Arrange the zucchini slices on the pan, slightly overlapping so they will all fit. Roast for about 20 minutes, checking once halfway through roasting. If the end slices are browning too quickly, exchange them for slices in the center of the pan. Let stand in the pan until ready to layer in the baking dish.

2 In a small bowl, combine the panko, Parmigiano-Reggiano, lemon zest, and salt and pepper to taste. Stir to blend and set aside. Spread the tomatoes on a plate and sprinkle with the basil.

3 Lightly oil the bottom and sides of a deep 2-quart baking dish. Sprinkle the bottom with ⅓ cup of the panko mixture. Top with a layer of roasted zucchini slices. Sprinkle with ½ cup of the mozzarella. Add a layer of tomatoes and sprinkle with another ⅓ cup of the panko mixture. Repeat layering, making a total of three layers of zucchini and two of tomatoes, adding a sprinkling of panko and cheese between each layer and topping off with panko and cheese.

4 Bake, uncovered, until the cheese is melted and the edges begin to turn golden, about 30 minutes. Let cool slightly before cutting into servings.

Stovetop Ratatouille

Over the years I've prepared this iconic dish both oven-roasted and cooked on top of the stove. Either way, the results are always delicious. The version has three variations: one topped with melted cheese, one with eggs poached in the ratatouille, and one made with both cheese and eggs. You can always skip the variations and enjoy the ratatouille plain, as a side dish, or spooned over hot pasta, rice, or polenta. **MAKES 4 SERVINGS**

1½ to 2 pounds small eggplants, trimmed, partially peeled (in stripes like a zebra), and cut into ⅓-inch cubes (about 4 cups)

2 cups diced (¼-inch pieces) white onion

1 pound green and yellow zucchini, trimmed and cut into ³⁄₈-inch cubes (about 3 cups)

1 medium red bell pepper, cored, seeded, and cut into ¼-inch pieces (about 1 cup)

1 small fennel bulb, trimmed and cut into ¼-inch pieces (about 1 cup)

Extra-virgin olive oil

2 garlic cloves, finely chopped

1 dried hot red chile or ¼ teaspoon crushed red pepper flakes, or more to taste

½ teaspoon dried fennel seeds

2 pounds ripe red and/or yellow tomatoes, trimmed and coarsely chopped, or 1 can (28 ounces) plum tomatoes with their juices

1 teaspoon coarse salt, plus more to taste

Freshly ground black pepper

½ cup torn fresh basil leaves

1 teaspoon fresh rosemary leaves

1 teaspoon fresh thyme leaves

1 teaspoon fresh oregano leaves

1 Set the eggplant aside in a separate bowl. Combine the onion, zucchini, bell pepper, and fennel in another bowl.

2 Heat ¼ inch of oil in a large, deep skillet or sauté pan until hot enough to sizzle a piece of eggplant. Gradually add the eggplant to the hot oil. Cook, stirring, adding drizzles of more oil, if needed, until the eggplant is browned and tender, about 10 minutes. Use a slotted spoon to transfer the eggplant to a large bowl.

3 Add the onion, zucchini, bell pepper, and fennel to the hot oil remaining in the skillet and cook, stirring and adjusting the heat between medium and medium-high to keep the vegetables sizzling without burning, until all the vegetables are golden and tender, about 15 minutes. Stir in the garlic, chile pepper, and fennel seeds and cook for about 1 minute. Add the tomatoes, salt, and a generous grinding of black pepper and bring to a boil. Simmer, stirring, until the mixture is thickened, about 15 minutes.

4 Gather the basil, rosemary, thyme, and oregano on the cutting board and finely chop together. Stir into the ratatouille. Taste the ratatouille and add more salt, if needed.

5 Serve hot, cold, or at room temperature.

Variation
STOVETOP RATATOUILLE WITH MELTED CHEESE

Sprinkle the surface of the hot ratatouille with 1 cup shredded Comté, Raclette, Manchego, Teleme, Monterey Jack, or another nutty-tasting cheese with excellent melting properties. Cover and continue to heat the ratatouille over medium-low heat until the cheese melts.

Variation
STOVETOP RATATOUILLE WITH POACHED EGGS OR POACHED EGGS AND CHEESE

Reserve half of the chopped herbs. Bring the ratatouille, covered, to a gentle boil over medium-low heat. One at a time, break each of 4 eggs into a cup, make 4 indentations in the ratatouille with the back of a large spoon, and slip an egg into each indentation. If not adding the cheese, cover and cook over medium-low heat until the eggs are set, 8 to 10 minutes. If using the cheese, sprinkle with 1 cup shredded Comté, Raclette, Teleme, Monterey Jack, or another nutty-tasting cheese with excellent melting properties. Then cover and cook until the eggs are set, 8 to 10 minutes. Sprinkle with the reserved herb mixture.

Vegetarian Shepherd's Pie

A classic shepherd's pie becomes a medley of cut-up vegetables—mush-rooms, leeks, carrots, parsnips, turnips, and peas—nestled in a rich, wine-laced pureed vegetable sauce and topped with creamy buttermilk mashed potatoes. MAKES 4 SERVINGS

2 pounds baking (russet) potatoes, peeled and cut into 1-inch chunks

1 to 1½ cups buttermilk

4 tablespoons (½ stick) unsalted butter, cut into ½-inch pieces

Coarse salt

1½ cups chopped stemmed shiitake mushrooms (about 5 ounces)

1½ cups chopped (½-inch pieces) cremini mushrooms (about 5 ounces)

1½ cups sliced (¼-inch pieces) leeks

1½ cups sliced (¼-inch pieces) peeled carrot

1½ cups diced (½-inch pieces) parsnip

1½ cups diced (½-inch pieces) turnip

4 tablespoons extra-virgin olive oil

2 garlic cloves, chopped

2 teaspoons chopped fresh thyme leaves

Freshly ground black pepper

2 cups full-bodied red wine

1 to 1½ cups Roasted Vegetable Broth (page 120)

1 cup thawed frozen peas

2 tablespoons chopped fresh parsley

1 Place the potatoes in a medium sauce-pan and cover with water. Bring to a boil and cook over medium heat, covered, until tender, about 15 minutes. Drain the pota-toes and return to the saucepan. Add 1 cup of the buttermilk and the butter and, using a potato masher, mash the potatoes until smooth. If too thick, add more buttermilk, a few tablespoons at a time. Add salt to taste.

2 Set aside 1 cup each of the shiitakes, cremini, leeks, carrots, parsnips, and turnips to be used in step 5.

3 Heat 2 tablespoons of the oil in a large skillet and add the ½ cup each of the shiitakes, cremini, leeks, carrots, parsnips, and turnips, half of the garlic, half of the thyme, 1 teaspoon of salt, and a grinding of pepper. Cook, stirring, over medium-low heat until the vegetables are tender and a light golden, about 15 minutes. Add the wine, bring to a boil, and boil until reduced by half. Let cool slightly. Transfer to a food processor and blend until smooth, gradually adding 1 cup of the broth through the feed tube until the mixture is a smooth puree. Add more broth if the sauce is too thick.

4 Preheat the oven to 400°F.

5 Wipe out the skillet and add the remaining 2 tablespoons oil and the reserved 1 cup each of the shiitakes, cremini, leeks, carrots, parsnips, and turnips, the remaining half each of the garlic and thyme, a sprinkling of salt, and a grinding of pepper. Cook, stirring, until golden brown and tender, about 15 minutes. Add the peas and parsley. Stir the sauce into the vegetables and gently fold to combine. Spoon the sauced vegetables into a 9- or 10-inch deep-dish pie plate.

6 Spoon the potatoes in equally spaced mounds on top of the vegetables. Bake until the sauce is bubbly and the potatoes are browned, about 25 minutes.

Peanut Vegetable Stew

Ground nut or peanut stews made hearty with cut-up root vegetables and green leaves—similar to our collards—and enriched with peanut butter are popular throughout Ethiopia. These filling stews are spiced with a pungent blend called berbere (pronounced bari-barAY). Earthy, bold, and hot, it can contain more than a dozen ingredients, including exotics such as puya pepper and fenugreek and more familiar names like paprika, ginger, black pepper, coriander, cumin, and cinnamon. The good news is you can approximate your own blend, buy it in a well-stocked spice shop, or order it online (see Sources, page 308). MAKES 6 SERVINGS

3 tablespoons peanut oil or other vegetable oil

2 cups coarsely chopped onion

1 tablespoon finely chopped garlic

1 tablespoon finely chopped peeled fresh ginger

2 teaspoons berbere (see page 218)

1 teaspoon ground cumin

¼ teaspoon ground cayenne, or more to taste

1½ to 1¾ cups warm water

½ cup thick peanut butter, preferably freshly ground from a health food store

1 can (14.5 ounces) diced tomatoes with their juices

1 cup diced (½-inch pieces) butternut or other orange-fleshed winter squash

1 cup diced (½-inch pieces) peeled sweet potato

1 cup diced (½-inch pieces) peeled turnip

1 cup diced (½-inch pieces) peeled carrot

1 tablespoon chopped fresh jalapeño pepper or serrano chile

1½ teaspoons coarse salt

2 cups chopped (1-inch pieces) collards (tough stems removed)

½ cup raw unsalted peanuts

1 Heat 2 tablespoons of the oil in a large heavy Dutch oven until hot enough to sizzle a piece of onion. Add the onion, turn the heat to low, and cook, covered, until the onion is softened and straw-colored, 10 to 15 minutes. Add the garlic and ginger and cook, stirring, for about 5 minutes. Stir in the berbere, cumin, and cayenne and cook, stirring, for about 1 minute.

2 In a small bowl, whisk 1½ cups of the warm water and the peanut butter until blended. Add the peanut butter mixture and the tomatoes to the onion. Bring to a boil, stirring constantly. Reduce the heat to low and cook, uncovered, for about 10 minutes. Stir in the squash, sweet potatoes, turnips, carrots, and jalapeño. Add

1 teaspoon of the salt. Cook, covered, over medium-low heat until the vegetables are almost tender, about 20 minutes. If the mixture seems dry, add the remaining ¼ cup water. Stir in the collards and cook until all the vegetables and the collards are tender, about 10 minutes.

3 Heat the remaining 1 tablespoon oil in a small skillet. Add the peanuts and sauté, stirring, until dark golden brown. Lift from the oil with a slotted spoon, place on a folded paper towel, and blot. Sprinkle with the remaining ½ teaspoon salt. Sprinkle the peanuts on top of the hot stew and serve in deep bowls.

Berbere

To make your own berbere, here is a recipe loosely adapted from the award-winning chef and restaurateur, Ethiopian-born Marcus Samuelsson, from his impressive *The Soul of a New Cuisine*.

With a mortar and pestle or spice grinder, finely grind ½ teaspoon fenugreek seeds. In a small bowl, stir together the fenugreek, ¼ cup sweet paprika, 2 tablespoons ground red pepper (cayenne), 1 tablespoon salt, 1 teaspoon ground ginger, 1 teaspoon onion powder, ½ teaspoon ground cardamom, ½ teaspoon ground nutmeg, and ¼ teaspoon each garlic powder, ground cloves, ground cinnamon, and allspice. Store, refrigerated, in an airtight jar or other container for up to 3 months.

Spicy Stir-Fried Tofu with Oyster Mushrooms, Red Pepper, and Bok Choy

Tofu is best when marinated in a robustly flavored marinade. A useful technique is to press the excess moisture from the tofu before marinating, because it makes room for the tofu to absorb more of the marinade. At the top of the list of marinade ingredients is soy sauce, followed closely by rice vinegar and sesame oil. In this recipe, I add honey, which not only contributes a touch of sweetness but also aids in the browning, and a bit of chile paste to give it a kick. Coating the tofu in a light dusting of cornstarch is a trick that adds texture. The best oils for stir-frying are those that will not burn when heated to a high temperature. Avocado, peanut, and canola oils are the most popular. **MAKES 4 SERVINGS**

12 ounces firm tofu

2 tablespoons soy sauce

2 tablespoons unseasoned Japanese rice vinegar

1 tablespoon honey

2 teaspoons toasted sesame oil (see page 221)

1 teaspoon Chinese chile-garlic paste or other hot chile sauce such as Sriracha, or more to taste

2 tablespoons cornstarch

3 tablespoons avocado, peanut, or canola oil

1 cup diced (½-inch pieces) red bell pepper

8 ounces oyster mushrooms, including stems, cut into ½-inch pieces

1 garlic clove, grated

½ teaspoon grated peeled fresh ginger

2 heads baby bok choy, trimmed and cut crosswise into ½-inch pieces

2 tablespoons thinly sliced scallion, cut on the diagonal (green parts only)

1 Stand the block of tofu on end and cut it into two thick, evenly sized slabs. Place a kitchen towel on a work surface, place the tofu on the towel, and fold it over the tofu. Place a small cutting board on top of the towel and press on the tofu to release some of the moisture. Let stand for about 20 minutes. Cut the pressed tofu into ¾-inch squares.

2 In a large bowl, combine the soy sauce, vinegar, honey, sesame oil, and chile paste to make a marinade. Whisk to blend. Add

the tofu and, with a rubber spatula, gently turn to coat. Marinate, stirring once or twice, for about 30 minutes, or longer if desired.

3 Place a strainer over a bowl and drain the tofu, reserving the marinade. Spread the cornstarch on a large plate or a sheet of wax paper. Heat a large, heavy skillet or wok over high heat until hot enough to sizzle a drop of water. Add the avocado oil and heat until shimmering. Lightly coat the tofu with the cornstarch, shaking off the excess. Add to the hot oil, a few pieces at a time, and cook, turning until evenly browned, 2 to 3 minutes. Remove to a side dish as the tofu browns.

4 Once all the tofu has been cooked, add the bell pepper to the skillet and stir-fry for about 1 minute. Add the mushrooms, garlic, and ginger and stir-fry, adjusting the heat to maintain a steady sizzle, for about 1 minute. Add the bok choy and stir-fry just until crisp-tender, about 2 minutes more. Add the browned tofu and the reserved marinade. Stir once to combine. Spoon into a serving bowl and top with the scallions.

Toasted Sesame Oil

Amber in color and strongly aromatic, toasted sesame oil is pressed from toasted sesame seeds. It adds a delicious depth of flavor to recipes. Purchase it in small bottles and store in the refrigerator to avoid rancidity.

Green Bean Tagine with Manuka Raisins and Preserved Lemon

Sturdy green beans simmer in a gently spiced mixture of tomato puree, sautéed onion, ginger, and garlic. Serve with couscous, as is the tradition in Morocco, or with cooked rice, quinoa, or another grain. It's also delicious served with sweet or white potatoes. MAKES 4 SERVINGS

2 tablespoons extra-virgin olive oil

2 cups thinly sliced onion

2 teaspoons finely chopped peeled fresh ginger

1 garlic clove, minced

2 teaspoons sweet paprika

1 teaspoon toasted ground cumin seeds (see page 57, Step 1)

1 pound large (mature) fresh green beans, trimmed, cut into 2-inch lengths

2 cups pureed Roasted Plum Tomatoes (page 103) or pureed canned whole tomatoes

1 cinnamon stick

½ teaspoon coarse salt, or to taste

Pinch of cayenne or 1 small dried red chile

¼ cup manuka raisins (see box) or Thompson seedless raisins

2 tablespoons diced Moroccan Preserved Lemon (page 305), pulp and membranes removed (optional)

2 tablespoons finely chopped fresh cilantro (optional)

1 Heat the oil in a large, heavy skillet with a lid or a shallow stovetop casserole until hot enough to sizzle a sliver of onion. Add the onion and cook over low heat, covered, stirring occasionally, until the onions are very tender and a pale golden color, 10 to 15 minutes. Add the ginger and garlic and cook, stirring, for about 1 minute.

2 Stir in the paprika and cumin and heat, stirring, for about 30 seconds. Add the green beans, tomatoes, cinnamon stick, salt, and cayenne and bring to a gentle boil. Stir in the raisins. Cover and cook over low heat until the beans are tender, 20 to 30 minutes, depending on their size.

3 Sprinkle with the Moroccan Preserved Lemon and cilantro, if using. Spoon into bowls and serve.

Manuka Raisins

Manuka raisins are large, chewy, and sweet. The few completely edible tiny seeds within each raisin add a pleasant crunch. Grown mostly in central Asia (Uzbekistan is a typical source), they're exported to the United States and, although sometimes hard to find, are available in some natural foods stores and online (see Sources, page 308).

Butternut Squash Korma

In Indian cuisine the term *korma* indicates a braise. This recipe uses ground nuts and yogurt in the braising liquid to produce a rich, creamy, velvety sauce for the squash. Serve it with basmati rice. **MAKES 4 SERVINGS**

½ cup chopped raw unsalted cashews, plus ½ cup more for garnish

2 cups water

3 tablespoons plus 1 teaspoon ghee (see page 76) or vegetable oil

2 cups diced (½-inch pieces) onion

2 teaspoons minced peeled fresh ginger

1 teaspoon minced or grated garlic

2 teaspoons Madras curry powder (see page 279)

Pinch of ground cayenne pepper or crushed red pepper flakes, or to taste

1 tablespoon tomato paste

1 large butternut squash (about 2 pounds), peeled, seeded, and cut into ½-inch pieces (about 8 cups)

1 teaspoon thinly sliced jalapeño or other hot green chile pepper (optional)

1 cup plain whole-milk Greek-style yogurt

1 cup thawed frozen green peas

1 Puree the cashews and ½ cup of the water in a blender or food processor until smooth. Scrape into a small bowl. Rinse the blender jar or food processor bowl with 1 cup more water and add to the pureed cashews in the bowl. Cover and let stand until ready to use.

2 Heat 3 tablespoons of the ghee in a large, deep skillet or sauté pan. Add the onion and cook, stirring, over medium-low heat until the onion is softened and begins to brown on the edges, 8 to 10 minutes. Reduce the heat to low. Stir in the ginger, garlic, curry powder, and cayenne and cook, stirring constantly, for about 1 minute.

3 In a small bowl, whisk together the tomato paste and remaining ½ cup water until the tomato paste is dissolved. To the skillet, add the squash, the cashew mixture, the tomato paste mixture, and the jalapeño (if using) and stir to combine. Cook, covered, over medium-low heat, stirring once or twice, until the squash is fork-tender, 15 to 20 minutes. Add the yogurt and peas and stir until blended. Cook over low heat, stirring gently, to warm the yogurt, 1 to 2 minutes. Do not boil.

4 Heat the remaining 1 teaspoon ghee in a small skillet and stir in the remaining ½ cup cashews. Cook, stirring, until lightly browned, about 3 minutes. Sprinkle over the korma and serve.

Eggplant and Egg Parmigiano

I loved my mother's southern Italian eggplant Parmigiano. She fried the slices in olive oil until they were dark brown and drenched in oil. Then to make what she considered a vegetable side dish into a main dish, she layered the eggplant with tomato sauce, shredded mozzarella, and sliced hard-cooked eggs. (She sometimes slipped in strips of salami to appease my father, a dedicated carnivore.) Jumping off from the hard-cooked egg idea, I've stacked the eggplant (oven baked, to cut the amount of oil) with roasted tomato sauce and cheese and then placed a gently cooked fried egg on top of each stack. Nestled in this gooey goodness, the yolk sets and the cheese melts when baked. This is best made with the Roasted Plum Tomatoes on page 103, but in a pinch you could use your favorite jarred sauce or canned crushed tomatoes. MAKES 4 TO 6 SERVINGS

2 medium eggplants (12 to 15 ounces each), trimmed, partially peeled (in stripes, like a zebra), and sliced ⅓ inch thick

Coarse salt

3 cups Roasted Plum Tomatoes (page 103), your favorite jarred tomato sauce, or canned crushed tomatoes

Extra-virgin olive oil

6 large eggs

6 ounces (about 1½ cups) shredded mozzarella cheese

½ cup grated Parmigiano-Reggiano

6 tablespoons combined chopped fresh flat-leaf (Italian) parsley, mint, and/or basil, or to taste

1 Layer the eggplant slices in a colander, sprinkling each layer lightly with salt. Set the colander over a large bowl, place a plate on top of the eggplant, and weight it with something heavy, such as a small iron skillet or a large can of tomatoes. Let stand for at least 1 hour. Place the colander in the sink and rinse off the salt. Lay the eggplant slices on a large kitchen towel and blot dry.

2 Meanwhile, puree the Roasted Plum Tomatoes in a food processor. Set aside for later. (If substituting jarred sauce or canned tomatoes, skip this step.)

3 Preheat the oven to 400°F. Brush two large baking sheets with a thin layer of oil and arrange the eggplant in a single layer, turning to lightly coat each slice with the oil. (For easy cleanup, the baking sheets

can be lined with parchment paper.) Roast for about 20 minutes. Turn the slices over and roast until browned, about 15 minutes more. Set aside. Reduce the oven temperature to 350°F.

4 Heat a large skillet over medium-high heat. Brush lightly with oil and when hot enough, break the eggs one at a time into a small cup and slip into the skillet. Fry the eggs over medium heat until the whites are set but the yolks are still runny, about 5 minutes. The eggs will be undercooked.

5 Spoon about 1 cup of the tomato sauce into the bottom of a large round 10-inch baking dish or an 8-x-10-inch rectangular baking dish and spread to the edges.

Arrange 6 of the largest eggplant slices in the pan. Sprinkle with ½ cup of the mozzarella and then a sprinkling of the Parmigiano. Sprinkle the cheese with half of the herbs. Top with the remaining eggplant, aligning them to make individual stacks, if possible. Double up on the smaller rounds of eggplant for each stack if necessary. Spoon 1 cup of the sauce over the top. Place a fried egg on top of each eggplant stack. Top with ½ cup more mozzarella and sprinkle with the remaining herbs. Top with the remaining sauce (a scant 1 cup) and the remaining ½ cup mozzarella. Sprinkle with any remaining Parmigiano.

6 Bake until the cheese is melted and the sauce is bubbly, about 20 minutes.

Shakshuka

Tunisian in origin, shakshuka is eaten widely throughout the Middle East and worldwide in restaurants and kitchens wherever Middle Eastern food is served. It is a favorite brunch dish, but being partial to eggs any time of the day, I love it for dinner, especially served in wide bowls with the sauce and eggs spooned over thick slices of olive oil–drizzled toasted crusty bread. MAKES 4 SERVINGS

¼ cup extra-virgin olive oil

1 red bell pepper, cut lengthwise into ⅛-inch-wide strips

1 Anaheim pepper, cut lengthwise into ⅛-inch-wide strips

1 medium onion, halved lengthwise, cut into thin slices

1½ teaspoons ground cumin

1 garlic clove, grated

1 large can (28 ounces) crushed tomatoes

2 teaspoons harissa (see page 72) or ¼ teaspoon crushed red pepper flakes, or to taste

2 tablespoons finely chopped fresh mint leaves

2 tablespoons finely chopped fresh dill

2 tablespoons finely chopped fresh cilantro

2 tablespoons diced Moroccan Preserved Lemon rinds (optional; page 305)

Coarse salt

4 large eggs

½ cup crumbled feta cheese (see page 62)

4 thick slices rustic bread, toasted and drizzled with olive oil, for serving

1 Heat the oil in a deep 10- to 12-inch skillet with a tight-fitting lid. Add the peppers and onion and cook, stirring occasionally, over medium heat until the vegetables are golden and softened, about 10 minutes. Add the cumin and garlic and cook, stirring, for about 1 minute.

2 Add the tomatoes, harissa, and half of the herbs. Bring to a gentle boil and cook over low heat, covered, for about 10 minutes. Add the preserved lemon, if using. Taste and add salt, if needed.

3 About 10 minutes before serving, break the eggs, one at a time, into a small bowl and slip them into the simmering sauce, spacing them evenly. Sprinkle with the feta. Cover and cook until the whites are set and the yolks are soft-set, 6 to 8 minutes, or longer for hard-cooked yolks.

4 To serve, place the toast in soup plates and ladle some of the tomato sauce over each. Top with an egg and sprinkle with the remaining half of the herbs.

Persian Herb Omelet

Traditionally made for the Persian New Year, this herb omelet, called *kuku*, is a much-loved dish that combines eggs, spices, handfuls of mint, dill, and parsley, and a most unlikely addition of baking powder, which gives the egg a pleasant spongy texture. I have added a small amount of grated Parmigiano-Reggiano to brown the top as the omelet finishes cooking under the broiler. Serve in wedges as a main course, or cut into small squares, skewer with fancy toothpicks, and serve as a snack.

MAKES 4 TO 8 SERVINGS

2 tablespoons unsalted butter

2 tablespoons extra-virgin olive oil

3 cups sliced (¼-inch pieces) trimmed leeks, including about 1 inch of the pale green tops

1 garlic clove, grated or finely chopped

1 teaspoon turmeric

½ teaspoon ground cumin

¼ teaspoon crushed saffron threads

8 large eggs

½ cup lightly packed chopped fresh mint leaves

½ cup lightly packed chopped fresh dill, including tender stems

½ cup lightly packed fresh flat-leaf (Italian) parsley, including tender stems

⅓ cup milk or half-and-half

2 tablespoons coarse dry bread crumbs

2 teaspoons baking powder

1 teaspoon coarse salt

Freshly ground black pepper

½ cup grated Parmigiano-Reggiano or shredded mozzarella

¼ cup thinly sliced green scallion tops (optional)

1 Heat a 9- or 10-inch ovenproof skillet over medium-high heat until hot enough to sizzle a drop of water. Add the butter and oil and swirl along the bottom and up the sides of the pan to coat.

2 Add the leeks and cook, stirring, over medium-low heat until wilted but still bright green, about 5 minutes. Add the garlic, turmeric, cumin, and saffron and cook, stirring, for about 1 minute. Remove from the heat.

3 Combine the eggs, mint, dill, parsley, milk, bread crumbs, baking powder, salt, and a grinding of pepper in a blender jar or food processor. Pulse until the herbs are chopped and the eggs are well blended.

continued >

4 Return the skillet to medium heat and cook until the leeks begin to sizzle, about 2 minutes. Add the egg mixture all at once. Cover and cook over medium-low heat until the edges begin to set, about 5 minutes. Uncover, tilt the pan, and lift the set egg with the edge of a rubber spatula to allow the liquid center to flow to the edges. Repeat around the edges of the omelet. Cover and cook over medium-low heat, adjusting the heat as needed to prevent the omelet from browning too quickly on the bottom, until the omelet is almost set, 15 to 20 minutes.

5 Heat the broiler and position the rack so that the top of the omelet is about 3 inches from the heat source. Spread the cheese on the top of the omelet and broil just until browned and bubbly, about 3 minutes.

6 Sprinkle with the scallions, if using. Let cool in the pan. Loosen the edges with a rubber spatula, pushing it under the omelet to make sure it isn't sticking to the bottom. Slide onto a serving platter or a cutting board and cut into portions. Serve warm, at room temperature, or cold.

RICE AND GRAINS

Basmati Rice with Caramelized Yellow Onions

I published a version of this glorious rice dish in my first rice cookbook, *The Amazing World of Rice*. This scaled-down adaptation uses turmeric instead of saffron to turn the crusty caramelized onions bright yellow. It's a perfect party dish served with cooked leafy greens and bean side dishes or with the Eggplant Balls in Pomegranate Tomato Sauce on page 190. The dish is especially beautiful when it turns out of the pan to form a cake crowned with caramelized onions. Don't despair if the onions stick to the bottom of the pan. The rice can be easily patted into place and the onions lifted from the pan with a rubber spatula and spread on top. The generous amount of butter is important. I've tried to make it with less, but it isn't quite the same. **MAKES 4 TO 6 SERVINGS**

1½ cups white basmati rice

4 whole cardamom pods

2 teaspoons coarse salt, plus more as needed

2 whole cloves

1 slice (¼ inch wide) fresh ginger

1 cinnamon stick

6 tablespoons (¾ stick) unsalted butter

2½ cups thinly sliced onion

½ teaspoon turmeric

Freshly ground black pepper

1 Bring a large saucepan half filled with water (about 2 quarts) to a boil. Add the rice, cardamom, salt, cloves, ginger, and cinnamon stick and cook, stirring occasionally, uncovered, until the rice is almost tender, about 15 minutes. Strain and set the rice aside. Leave all of the spices in the rice. Taste the rice and sprinkle with more salt, if needed.

2 Meanwhile, heat 2 tablespoons of the butter in a 10-inch heavy well-seasoned or nonstick skillet until foaming. Add the onions and cook, stirring, over medium-low heat, until the onions are golden, about 15 minutes. Add the turmeric and a generous grinding of pepper and stir until the onions are evenly colored. Spread the

onions in a thin, even layer to the edges of the skillet. Leave the skillet on the stove over low heat.

3 With a large spoon, add one rounded spoonful of the rice (including the spices) at a time to the skillet, using the back of the spoon to gently press the rice evenly over the onions with each addition. Cut the remaining 4 tablespoons butter into small bits and scatter on top of the rice. Smooth the top with the back of a spoon and press down so the rice will form a cake. Cut a piece of foil about an inch larger than the diameter of the skillet. Place on top of the rice and press down firmly with the back of a spoon. Place a smaller lid on top of the foil so it can be pressed down during cooking.

4 Cook the rice over medium-low to low heat, pressing the cover down on the foil frequently, for about 20 minutes. Lift the cover and peek under the foil. The rice around the edges of the pan should be golden when moved aside with the tip of a knife. If not, re-cover with the foil and the lid and cook over low heat for 5 to 10 minutes longer.

5 Turn off the heat and let the rice rest for 10 minutes. Remove the lid and the foil. Run the edge of a rubber spatula along the edges to loosen the rice from the pan. Invert a large, round, flat plate onto the surface of the rice. Wearing oven mitts, quickly invert the skillet onto the plate. The onions should be dark brown to golden and the rice along the sides of the pan crusty.

Summer Garden Paella

Vegetable paella with the typical flavor components—paprika, sautéed onion, bell peppers, tomatoes, and garlic—is becoming more and more popular. For this seasonal version, wedges of ripe tomato, fragrant basil, diced zucchini, and crunchy corn kernels add the fresh taste of summer. The best rice for paella is the short-grain type—Italian Arborio or Spanish Bomba, Calasparra, and Valencia—which swell and absorb all the delicious seasonings in the broth. The rice in paella is always cooked soft and moist, not dry and separate as in a pilaf-style dish. After removing the pan from the oven, let it stand over low heat to give the grains along the bottom of the pan a chance to brown. Called *socarrat*, this golden crust is considered a delicacy. MAKES 4 SERVINGS

4 cups Roasted Vegetable Broth (page 120) or half broth and half water, plus more as needed

6 medium tomatoes (about 1½ pounds), cored and cut into ½-inch wedges

1 medium zucchini (about 6 ounces), trimmed and cut into ¼-inch cubes

¼ cup extra-virgin olive oil

3 tablespoons chopped fresh basil

1½ teaspoons coarse salt

Freshly ground black pepper

1 cup diced (¼-inch pieces) onion

½ cup diced (¼-inch pieces) red bell pepper

1 garlic clove, crushed with the side of a knife and chopped

2 teaspoons smoked paprika, preferably pimentón de la Vera (see page 26)

1½ cups Arborio, Bomba, or other short-grain rice

1 tablespoon tomato paste

1½ cups fresh corn kernels (from 2 ears)

1 In a saucepan, bring the broth to a boil; keep the broth hot over low heat. In a medium bowl, combine the tomatoes, zucchini, 2 tablespoons of the oil, and 2 tablespoons of the basil; sprinkle with ½ teaspoon of the salt and a generous grinding of pepper. Toss to coat.

2 Heat the remaining 2 tablespoons oil in a 10- or 12-inch ovenproof skillet or stovetop-to-oven casserole over medium-high heat until hot enough to sizzle a piece of onion. Add the onion and bell pepper and cook, stirring, until the vegetables are golden, 10 to 15 minutes. Add the garlic and cook over low heat, stirring occasionally, for

about 30 seconds. Add the paprika and cook, stirring, for another 30 seconds.

3 Add the rice and tomato paste and cook over low heat, stirring, until the rice is coated with the seasonings. Add the hot broth and the remaining 1 teaspoon salt and bring to a boil. Boil over medium heat, covered, for about 10 minutes. Uncover and stir in the corn and the remaining 1 table-spoon basil.

4 Preheat the oven to 400°F. Spoon the tomato and zucchini mixture on top of the partially cooked rice and pour the tomato juices on top. Bake, uncovered, for about 20 minutes. Remove the pan from the oven and taste the rice. If it is still very firm or if the mixture is dry, add ½ to 1 cup boiling water.

5 Raise the oven temperature to 450°F. Return the pan to the oven and bake until all of the moisture is absorbed and the rice is tender, 10 to 15 minutes longer. Remove the pan from the oven and place on the stove-top over medium-low to low heat. Cook for 10 to 15 minutes to allow the rice on the bottom of the pan to brown before serving.

Evan's Jamaican Rice and Peas

Brought to Jamaica through the slave trade, the peas in this dish are not the fresh plump garden peas familiar to all of us, but the small round dried peas that come in a variety of colors from ivory to pale green to dark red. This iconic dish of rice and peas is from the kitchen of Evan Elder, the son of my good friends Pam and Desmond Elder (Desmond grew up in Jamaica), where rice and peas—including this version made with luscious coconut milk, dried thyme, and a subtle hint of curry powder—is a favorite. Evan, who has perfected his father's recipe, prefers fiery habanero chiles, but I prefer small green serranos, which while being less authentic are also not as hot. Pigeon peas are grown in the American South and in some regions can be purchased fresh, dried, frozen, or canned.

MAKES 6 TO 8 SERVINGS

- 1 pound small dried pigeon peas or small round red beans, rinsed and sorted
- 2 cans (13.5 ounces each) coconut milk
- 2 tablespoons sugar
- 1 tablespoon dried thyme
- 4 to 5 teaspoons coarse salt
- ½ teaspoon Madras curry powder (see page 279)
- 2½ cups long-grain white rice
- 1 cup sliced scallion (green and white parts; about 2 bunches)
- 1 habanero pepper or other spicy chile pepper, or more to taste

1 Place the beans in a 4-quart saucepan and add enough water to cover by about 1 inch. Bring to a boil, reduce the heat, and simmer, checking the water level frequently and adding more water as needed. The water level should just cover the beans by about ½ inch throughout the cooking time. Cook, covered, until the beans are tender, 1½ to 2½ hours depending on the age of the beans.

2 Preheat the oven to 350°F. Place a colander over a bowl and drain the beans, reserving the liquid separately. Pour the coconut milk into an 8-cup measure and add enough of the reserved bean cooking liquid to make 6½ cups liquid total. (Add water if there is not enough cooking liquid, or discard the unused cooking liquid if you have more than you need.)

3 Combine the coconut-water mixture, sugar, thyme, 4 teaspoons salt, and curry powder in a 6-quart Dutch oven and bring to a boil. Reduce the heat and simmer for

about 5 minutes. Add the beans, rice, scallions, and chile pepper and bring to a boil. Stir thoroughly and cover.

4 Transfer the Dutch oven to the oven and bake for 20 minutes. Remove from the oven (the dish will require longer cooking) and taste the rice. If it needs more salt, stir about 1 teaspoon salt into ¼ cup warm tap water in a small cup until dissolved. Sprinkle over the rice and beans. Find the chile pepper and transfer to a small bowl. Pull off and discard the stem. Mash the chile with the back of a fork and add the mashed chile and its juices to the rice. Gently fold the mixture to incorporate the salt water (if using) and the chile. Return the pot to the oven and bake until all the liquid is absorbed, the beans and rice are tender, and the edges are beginning to brown, about 25 minutes longer.

5 Let the rice cool on top of the stove for at least 20 minutes. The dish improves when refrigerated overnight. To reheat, spoon into a microwavable or ovenproof serving dish, and reheat in the microwave or place the covered dish in a 350°F oven until the rice and peas are heated through. Do not stir, or the rice will turn sticky.

Kimchi Fried Rice

This recipe is based loosely on the more typical Chinese fried rice, but the addition of kimchi makes it Korean-esque. I love it, especially with scrambled egg added at the end. (Fried cubes of tofu are good, too.) It's a great-tasting, quick, and easy supper dish, especially if you have some cold cooked rice on hand to get you started right away. **MAKES 4 SERVINGS**

3 cups cold leftover cooked short-grain brown or white rice

4 tablespoons peanut or vegetable oil

¼ cup unsalted raw peanuts

¼ cup chopped onion

½ cup finely chopped or shredded peeled carrot

1 garlic clove, grated

1 teaspoon grated peeled fresh ginger

2 large eggs, beaten (optional)

½ cup coarsely chopped Vegetarian Kimchi (page 133)

Sriracha or other favorite hot sauce, for serving (optional)

1 The rice must be cold for the grains to remain separate; if it is warm, the rice will clump and stick. If you need to cook the rice just before making fried rice, quicken the cooling process by spreading the cooked rice on a baking sheet and refrigerating until cold.

2 Heat a wok or large, heavy skillet over high heat until searing hot. Add 2 tablespoons of the oil and the peanuts and turn the heat to medium-low. Stir until the peanuts begin to brown, about 2 minutes. Immediately remove the peanuts with a slotted spoon or a skimmer and place on a paper towel–lined dish. Let cool and then finely chop.

3 Add the onion to the hot oil and stir-fry over medium heat until translucent, about 5 minutes. Add the carrot, garlic, and ginger and stir-fry for about 1 minute. Add the rice and turn the heat back up to high. With the back of a spoon pack the rice onto the sides of the wok so it can toast slightly. Then, with a large round spoon, lift the rice from the pan and turn to brown more surfaces, and cook, adding drizzles of the remaining 2 tablespoons oil as needed, for about 5 minutes.

4 If using the eggs, clear a spot in the middle of the wok and add a tiny drizzle of oil. When the oil is hot, add the eggs all at once and stir slowly with a fork or a chopstick until it is cooked into clumps. Add the kimchi and stir it into the rice. Cook for about 3 minutes. Top with the peanuts. Serve with the hot sauce, if desired.

Coconut Milk Rice Pilaf
with Cilantro Sauce

This is an especially fragrant rice pilaf that is best made with imported basmati rice, which elongates into slender grains as it cooks. The rice is first rinsed in cold water, to remove the excess starch, as is the tradition in India. The pilaf is very good without the drizzle of Cilantro Sauce, but adding the pale green, tangy sauce makes it even better. **MAKES 4 SERVINGS**

Pilaf

- 1 cup basmati rice, preferably imported
- 2 tablespoons ghee (see page 76) or coconut oil
- 3 whole cloves
- 3 green or white cardamom pods
- 1 bay leaf
- 1 cinnamon stick
- ½ teaspoon cumin seeds
- 1 can (13.5 ounces) coconut milk (about 1¾ cups)
- About ¼ cup water
- 1 teaspoon coarse salt, or to taste

Cilantro Sauce

- ½ cup plain whole-milk yogurt
- ½ cup packed coarsely chopped fresh cilantro, leaves and tender stems
- 1 to 2 teaspoons minced jalapeño, to taste

1 Make the pilaf: Place the rice in a bowl and add water to cover. Swirl the water around with a chopstick or the handle of a wooden spoon for about 20 seconds. Strain and discard the water. Set the rice aside.

2 Heat the ghee in a large, deep skillet with a lid until hot. Add the cloves, cardamom, bay leaf, cinnamon stick, and cumin and heat, stirring, for about 30 seconds. Add the rice and stir to coat with the ghee; cook over medium heat until the rice grains begin to turn white, about 1 minute.

3 Pour the coconut milk into a large measuring cup and whisk in enough water to measure 2 cups. Add the coconut milk–water mixture to the rice and bring to a boil. Add the salt and stir once, thoroughly. Cover and cook over medium-low heat until the coconut milk has been absorbed and the rice grains are separate, about 12 minutes. Do not stir. Remove from the heat. Cover and let stand, without stirring, for 10 minutes.

4 Make the Cilantro Sauce: While the rice is cooking, combine the yogurt, cilantro, and jalapeño in a food processor and puree until smooth (there will be tiny flecks of green throughout the yogurt).

5 Spoon the pilaf into a serving dish and drizzle the Cilantro Sauce on top.

Farrotto with Broccolini and Parmigiano-Reggiano

It is hard to pass a prepared salad bar without sighting a salad made with farro. Farro, also known as emmer wheat, is a round, chewy ancient grain with a mild flavor similar to that of barley. Look for packages that say semi-perlato, which means the bran has been scraped to hasten the cooking time. Here it is paired with broccolini or broccoli rabe in a dish similar to risotto. **MAKES 4 SERVINGS**

1 bay leaf

1 garlic clove, bruised with the side of a knife, plus 1 clove, grated

1½ cups semi-perlato farro

2 teaspoons coarse salt

3 to 4 cups Roasted Vegetable Broth (page 120)

1 bunch (about 8 ounces) broccolini or 1 bunch (about 1 pound) broccoli rabe

3 tablespoons extra-virgin olive oil

½ cup chopped onion

Pinch of crushed red pepper flakes

½ cup grated Parmigiano-Reggiano, plus curls for garnish

1 Bring a large, wide saucepan half filled with water plus the bay leaf and bruised garlic clove to a boil. Stir in the farro and salt. Bring back to a boil and cook, stirring occasionally, over medium-high heat until the farro is close to tender, 20 to 25 minutes. Drain the farro. Discard the bay leaf. The garlic will have mostly disintegrated.

2 Heat the broth in a small saucepan to a simmer. Cover the saucepan and keep the broth hot over low heat.

3 Meanwhile, prepare the broccolini. Trim the tips from the stalks and discard. Gather the stalks together on a cutting board and cut into ½-inch pieces. When you get to the blossoms cut across only once or twice as they fall away into short stems. You should have about 4 cups cut-up broccolini. Set aside.

4 Rinse and dry the saucepan used to cook the farro. Heat the oil in the pan until hot enough to sizzle a piece of onion. Add the onion and cook, stirring, over medium-low heat until the onion is golden, about 5 minutes. Remove from the heat and stir in the grated garlic and the red pepper flakes.

5 Add the broccolini to the onion mixture and toss to combine. Stir in the farro. Add 1 cup of the hot broth and cook the farro and broccolini over medium-high heat, stirring, until most of the broth is absorbed, about 5 minutes. Add another cup of broth and cook, stirring, until absorbed, about 5 minutes. Continue cooking, stirring, and adding broth until the farro is soft, the broccolini is cooked, and the farrotto is thick but very moist, about 10 minutes. Stir in the grated cheese.

6 Spoon the farrotto into individual wide, shallow soup bowls and sprinkle each serving with curls of the Parmigiano-Reggiano.

Mushroom Chilaquiles

Tortillas are the bread of Mexico. Consequently, there are many recipes in the Mexican repertoire that use day-old, or yesterday's, tortillas. One popular preparation with a rather playful-sounding name is chilaquiles. The most popular version, a favorite brunch or breakfast dish, is a simple combination of fried day-old torn tortilla topped with melted cheese, fried or scrambled eggs, and salsa. This version without eggs uses mushrooms in the sauce, which has been robustly layered with heat from three different types of chiles. Rather than tomato puree, I use canned plum tomatoes in juice that are whirled in the food processor until coarsely chopped or pressed through a food mill. This is a festive, filling, and fun dish to serve for breakfast or brunch, lunch or dinner. MAKES 4 SERVINGS

1 poblano chile

8 ounces mushrooms, such as cremini, shiitake, and/or portobello

¼ cup extra-virgin olive oil

½ medium onion, thinly sliced

1 tablespoon finely chopped jalapeño pepper

1 garlic clove, grated or finely chopped

1 teaspoon coarse salt

1 teaspoon dried Mexican oregano (see page 110) or Italian oregano

1 large can (28 ounces) plum tomatoes with their juices, pureed in a food processor or through a food mill

1 teaspoon minced chipotle in adobo sauce (see page 130)

8 (6-inch) day-old corn tortillas

Vegetable oil, for the tortillas, as needed

½ cup shredded Oaxaca or Chihuahua cheese (see page 249), mozzarella, or Monterey Jack cheese

½ cup crumbled cotija (see page 249) or feta cheese (see page 62)

1 large ripe avocado, peeled, pitted, and cut into thin wedges

½ seedless cucumber, peeled and thinly sliced

6 radishes, thinly sliced

1 lime, cut into wedges

½ cup coarsely chopped fresh cilantro leaves and tender stems

Mexican crema (see page 249) or sour cream, for serving

1 Preheat the broiler, placing the rack so that the poblano will be about 2 inches from the heat source. Place the poblano chile on a sheet of foil and place it on a baking sheet. Broil, turning once or twice, until the skin is evenly blistered, about 5 minutes per side. Remove from the broiler and wrap the poblano in the foil. Let stand

until cool enough to handle. Once cool, unwrap and carefully pull off the charred skin. Cut the poblano in half, remove and discard the stem and seeds, and coarsely chop the flesh.

2 If using shiitakes, cut off and discard the tough stems. Heat the oil in a large, deep skillet until hot enough to sizzle a piece of mushroom. Add the mushrooms and onion and cook, stirring, over medium heat until the onions are limp and the mushrooms begin to brown, 8 to 10 minutes. Add the jalapeño, garlic, salt, and oregano and cook over medium-low heat, stirring, for about 1 minute. Add the tomatoes, reserved poblano, and chipotle and bring to a boil. Reduce the heat to medium-low and cook the sauce until thickened, about 15 minutes.

3 While the sauce is simmering, prepare the tortillas. **For fried tortillas:** Stack the tortillas and cut into 1-inch squares. Heat about ½ inch of vegetable oil in a skillet until hot enough to sizzle a piece of tortilla. Add half of the tortilla pieces and fry, stirring carefully with a large fork, until crisp and a shade darker, about 3 minutes. With a slotted spoon, remove to a large strainer set over a bowl or to layers of paper towels spread on a tray. Repeat with the remaining tortillas. **Alternatively, for baked tortillas:** Preheat the oven to 375°F. Lightly brush the whole tortillas on one side with vegetable oil. Stack the tortillas and cut into 1-inch squares. Spread the tortillas on one or two baking sheets and bake until crisp, stirring once, 12 to 15 minutes.

4 Just before serving, stir half of the crisp tortillas into the sauce and cook, stirring, for about 2 minutes. If the sauce isn't thickened, stir in the remaining tortillas, but if the sauce appears to be thick enough, serve the remaining tortillas as a snack.

5 Spoon the chilaquiles onto a large deep platter. Sprinkle the Oaxaca cheese and cotija over the top and garnish the edges with the avocado, cucumber, radishes, and lime wedges. Sprinkle the cilantro over the top. Serve with Mexican crema in a bowl on the side or drizzled over the top.

Mexican Cheese (and Other Dairy)

Crema This is Mexican cream that is thick and slightly sour, reminiscent of the French crème fraîche. Plain sour cream thinned with a little milk can be substituted.

Añejo Cheese (Queso de Añejo) This is a hard, salty, aged cow's-milk cheese that is best grated or crumbled. (It is sometimes sold grated.) Asiago or Pecorino Romano are suitable substitutes.

Cotija Cheese Similar to añejo, cotija is a pungent, aged, salty cheese that is most often crumbled on top of dishes. It softens rather than melts. Substitute feta.

Queso Fresco Translated as "fresh cheese," this is a salty, moist cheese with a crumbly texture. Ricotta salata, salted farmer cheese, or a mild French feta are good substitutes.

Panela, Asadero, and Chihuahua Cheese (Queso de Asadero, Queso de Chihuahua) These are all mild-tasting moist cheeses, often used as melting cheeses. Teleme, mozzarella, Monterey Jack, or Muenster can be substituted. Panela is sold molded in a basket.

Oaxaca Cheese (Queso de Oaxaca) Considered the mozzarella of Mexico, this cheese is most often found in a round twist enclosed in shrink-wrap. It is an excellent melting cheese. Look for small balls, which make a great snack.

Requesón Cheese (Queso de Requesón) Often called Mexican "ricotta," this cheese has soft creamy curds. Substitute whole-milk Italian ricotta.

Baked Tortilla Casserole

Popularly known as *sopa seca*, or dry soup, this is a baked variation of the popular breakfast and brunch dish called chilaquiles (page 246). I think of it more as the Mexican version of the Italian lasagna: gooey and delicious. It's a great way to use up leftover day-old corn tortillas. **MAKES 6 TO 8 SERVINGS**

1 poblano chile

2 teaspoons whole cumin seeds

2 tablespoons extra-virgin olive oil

½ cup chopped onion

2 garlic cloves, finely chopped

1 large can (28 ounces) crushed tomatoes

1 can (15 ounces) tomato sauce

2 teaspoons chopped chipotle in adobo sauce (see page 130)

Vegetable oil, as needed for frying the tortillas

12 (6-inch) day-old corn tortillas, cut into 1-inch-wide strips

1 cup (about 6 ounces) crumbled queso fresco (see page 249), salted farmer cheese, or mild feta (see page 62)

8 ounces Oaxaca or Chihuahua cheese (see page 249) or other soft melting cheese, such as mozzarella or Monterey Jack, cut into thin slivers

1 cup Mexican crema (see page 249) or sour cream

1 Preheat the broiler and position the rack about 3 inches from the heat source. Line a sheet pan with foil and place the poblano on the foil. Broil, turning the pepper as it blisters and chars, 5 minute per side. Remove from the broiler and wrap in the foil. Once cool, unwrap and rub off the charred skin. Split the poblano in half and remove and discard the stem and seeds. Coarsely chop the flesh and set aside.

2 Place the cumin seeds in a small skillet and heat, shaking the pan, until the seeds are a shade darker, 2 to 3 minutes. Let cool and then grind in a spice grinder or pound in a mortar with a pestle. You should have 2 teaspoons ground. Set aside.

3 Heat the olive oil in a wide, deep pot or Dutch oven over medium-low heat until hot enough to sizzle a piece of onion. Add the onion and cook, stirring, until golden, about 8 minutes. Add the garlic and cook for about 1 minute. Stir in the cumin, crushed tomatoes, tomato sauce, reserved poblano, and chipotle and bring to a boil. Reduce the heat and simmer, uncovered, until slightly reduced, about 30 minutes.

4 Meanwhile, heat about 1 inch of vegetable oil in a large, heavy skillet until hot enough to sizzle a strip of tortilla. Add half of the tortillas and cook, stirring, until crisp, 3 to 5 minutes. Lift from the oil with tongs and let drain on a paper towel–lined baking sheet. Repeat with the remaining tortillas.

5 Preheat the oven to 350°F. Spread a layer of the tomato sauce in the bottom of a 3-quart casserole or soufflé dish. Top with a layer of tortilla chips, cheeses, and more tomato sauce. Repeat until all the tortilla strips are used, ending with a layer of sauce and then a layer of cheese.

6 Bake until hot and bubbly, about 45 minutes. Before serving, drizzle the casserole with the crema and serve any remaining crema on the side.

Bulgur Pilaf with Dried Apricots

Bulgur is the grain of choice throughout the Arab world, cooked in a variety of ways in soups, stews, and pilafs. This simple pilaf features dried apricots, but raisins are just as commonly used. Sautéed pignoli, almonds, or walnuts are a traditional topping. MAKES 4 TO 6 SERVINGS

½ cup pignoli

2 tablespoons extra-virgin olive oil

1 cup chopped onion

1 cinnamon stick (optional)

1½ cups medium or coarse bulgur (see page 170)

½ cup chopped dried apricots

2 cups water

1 teaspoon coarse salt

1 Heat a small, heavy skillet over medium heat until hot enough to sizzle a drop of water. Add the pignoli and toast, stirring constantly, over medium-low heat until golden, about 3 minutes. Set aside.

2 Heat the oil in a wide, deep skillet until hot enough to sizzle a piece of onion. Add the onion and the cinnamon stick, if using, and cook, stirring occasionally, until the onion is golden, about 5 minutes. Add the bulgur and apricots and stir to combine. Add the water and salt and bring to a boil. Stir well, cover, and cook, without stirring, until the water is absorbed, about 10 minutes. Let stand, covered and undisturbed, for 5 to 10 minutes. Spoon into a serving bowl and sprinkle with the toasted pignoli.

NOODLES AND PASTA

Thai Curried Rice Noodles with Dried Shiitake Mushrooms and Spinach

Making noodles tossed in a wok isn't that different from making stir-fried rice. I especially love the addition of the omelet "pancake" cut into thin strips, which resemble the noodles. Look for yellow or red Thai curry paste, which has a vibrant, fruity taste. The heat level fluctuates among the many different brands out there, so taste and adjust the amount as you make the stir-fry sauce for the noodles. You won't need an authentic wok to prepare this recipe. I use my wok-skillet, which I find easy to handle, but any large, heavy skillet will work as well. **MAKES 4 SERVINGS**

4 large dried shiitake mushrooms

8 ounces thin (about ⅛ inch wide) dried or fresh rice noodles

2 teaspoons toasted sesame oil (see page 221)

1 large egg, beaten

½ cup water or vegetable broth, plus 2 teaspoons water

2 tablespoons plus 1 teaspoon soy sauce, plus more for serving

1 tablespoon plus 1 teaspoon vegetable oil

2 tablespoons Chinese rice wine or sherry

1 to 3 tablespoons yellow or red curry paste, to taste

½ cup thinly sliced scallion (white and green parts), cut on the diagonal

1 tablespoon julienned peeled fresh ginger

1 teaspoon grated garlic

3 ounces baby spinach, rinsed and dried

1 Place the mushrooms in a small bowl, cover with boiling water, and soak until pliable, about 20 minutes. Drain. Cut out and discard the stems. Cut the caps into thin slices and place in the small bowl, add boiling water to cover, and soak for 20 minutes longer. Drain and reserve.

2 Prepare the noodles following the package instructions, soaking or boiling, as directed, until pliable. Drain well and toss with the sesame oil.

continued >

3 Beat the egg with the 2 teaspoons water and 1 teaspoon of the soy sauce. Heat the skillet or wok over high heat until hot enough to sizzle a drop of water. Add about 1 teaspoon of the vegetable oil and swirl the pan to coat. Add the egg mixture and cook, without stirring, but tilting the pan and lifting the edges of the egg as it sets so the raw center can flow under the set egg, about 1 minute. Carefully slide the egg from the skillet onto a small plate and let stand until cooled.

4 In a small bowl, stir together the remaining ½ cup water, the remaining 2 tablespoons soy sauce, the Chinese rice wine, and 1 tablespoon of the curry paste until blended. Taste and add more curry paste, if desired, until just slightly above your preferred heat level. (The noodles will temper the heat of the sauce in the finished dish.)

5 Reheat the skillet until hot enough to sizzle a drop of water. Add the remaining 1 tablespoon vegetable oil and heat until hot enough to sizzle a piece of scallion. Add the scallions, ginger, and garlic and stir-fry for about 20 seconds. Add the curry paste mixture and bring to a boil.

6 Drain the reserved mushrooms. Add the noodles, mushrooms, and spinach to the skillet and cook, stirring with chopsticks or tongs, until all the liquid is evenly absorbed and the spinach is wilted, about 3 minutes. Cut the egg into strips and strew over the top. Pass the soy sauce to sprinkle on each serving as needed.

Crisp Noodle Pancake with Stir-Fried Vegetables

Crunchy noodles topped with stir-fried vegetables harken from the days when we called cilantro coriander, and the word *Oriental* was the standard in recipe writing. Retro, for sure, but, here it is updated with fresh snow peas, baby bok choy, and Chinese broccoli, three vegetables we never saw in the distant past unless we were lucky enough to have a Chinese or an Asian market nearby. **MAKES 4 SERVINGS**

8 ounces fresh or dried Chinese egg noodles or thin spaghetti

2 teaspoons toasted sesame oil (see page 221)

2 tablespoons unseasoned Japanese rice vinegar

1 tablespoon plus 1 teaspoon tamari or soy sauce (see page 44)

2 teaspoons honey

2 teaspoons cornstarch

2 tablespoons vegetable oil

2 teaspoons grated peeled fresh ginger

1 garlic clove, grated

¼ teaspoon crushed red pepper flakes

1 bunch (about 1 pound) Chinese broccoli (*gai lan*), trimmed and cut into 1-inch pieces, or substitute broccolini or broccoli rabe

3 tablespoons water

4 heads baby bok choy, trimmed and cut crosswise into 1-inch pieces

1 cup snow peas, trimmed and cut on the diagonal into ½-inch pieces

2 scallions (white and green parts), cut on the diagonal into thin pieces

1 Cook the noodles in plenty of boiling salted water until al dente, or firm to the bite, 2 to 5 minutes; drain. Rinse with cold water and shake well in a colander. Spread on a kitchen towel and blot dry. Combine the noodles in a bowl with 1 teaspoon of the sesame oil and toss to coat. Set aside.

2 Stir together the remaining 1 teaspoon sesame oil, vinegar, tamari, honey, and cornstarch in a small bowl until blended to make a sauce.

3 Heat 1 tablespoon of the vegetable oil in a 10-inch skillet and add the noodles; spread in a flat layer. Cover and cook over medium heat, shaking the skillet once or twice to prevent sticking, until brown, about 5 minutes. Invert the skillet onto a flat inverted lid or a large plate and then slide back into the skillet, browned side up, and brown the other side, about 5 minutes more. Cover and keep warm while stir-frying the vegetables.

continued >

4 Meanwhile, heat a wok or another skillet over medium-high heat until hot enough to sizzle a drop of water. Add the remaining 1 tablespoon vegetable oil, ginger, garlic, and red pepper flakes and stir-fry for about 10 seconds. Add the Chinese broccoli and the water; cover and cook until crisp-tender, 3 to 5 minutes. Add the bok choy and snow peas and cook, stirring, until crisp-tender, about 1 minute. Add the sauce and cook, stirring, until the sauce thickens and coats the vegetables, 1 to 2 minutes. Stir in the scallions.

5 Slide the noodle pancake onto a plate and top with the vegetables.

Cold Chinese Noodles
with Peanut Sauce

This dish is a longtime family favorite. You can find Asian wheat noodles in many markets. If they are not available, you can use dried thin spaghetti or coils of dried Chinese noodles. **MAKES 4 SERVINGS**

16 ounces fresh thin Chinese wheat noodles

3 tablespoons toasted sesame oil (see page 221)

3 tablespoons Chinese sesame paste (see box) or tahini (see page 41)

2 tablespoons hot water

3 tablespoons soy sauce or tamari (see page 44)

3 tablespoons smooth peanut butter

2 tablespoons unseasoned Japanese rice vinegar

2 tablespoons honey

2 teaspoons Sriracha or Chinese chile-garlic paste, or to taste

1½ teaspoons grated peeled fresh ginger

¼ cup slivered scallion, cut lengthwise into 2-x-⅛-inch pieces (white and green parts)

½ cup slivered seedless cucumbers, cut lengthwise into 2-x-⅛-inch pieces

1 tablespoon tan sesame seeds (see page 60)

2 tablespoons finely chopped fresh cilantro (optional)

1 Cook the noodles in plenty of boiling salted water until firm to the bite, 2 to 5 minutes. Drain, rinse with cold water, and drain again, shaking off excess water.

Transfer the drained noodles to a large bowl. Add 1 tablespoon of the oil and toss with a fork or chopsticks to coat. Set aside until cool.

2 In a medium bowl, if using the Chinese sesame paste, combine it with the hot water and stir until the paste is dissolved. If using tahini as a substitute, add the tahini and the hot water, but it is not necessary to dissolve the tahini. Add the remaining 2 tablespoons oil, the soy sauce, peanut butter, vinegar, honey, Sriracha, and ginger; whisk until smooth.

3 Add the sauce to the cooled noodles and toss with chopsticks until the noodles are coated. Transfer to a shallow serving bowl and top with the scallions, cucumber, sesame seeds, and cilantro, if using. Serve at room temperature or chilled.

Chinese Sesame Paste

Chinese sesame paste, sold in Asian markets, is very different from tahini. It is the consistency of moist clay and must be softened in hot water before adding to dishes. Tahini may be substituted.

Pasta Gratin with Ricotta, Escarole, Acorn Squash, and Two Cheeses

A classic dish of pasta tossed with vegetables and cheese, this version uses creamy ricotta, whisked with some of the starchy pasta cooking water, as a "sauce." The vegetables can vary with the season. In the fall, I like to use diced pieces of winter squash and greens braised in olive oil with smashed garlic cloves, with ground cinnamon to flavor the ricotta. For a version without the winter squash, omit the cinnamon and add crushed red pepper flakes as a flavor note. For other variations, try adding some bits of sun-dried tomato or black olives, steamed florets of cauliflower or broccoli, fresh corn kernels, or chopped marjoram, savory, or basil. The dish is also excellent with mushrooms cooked in olive oil with garlic. Any shape pasta will do as well. Favorites are penne, penne rigate, spiral or corkscrew shapes, shells, or any number of others. **MAKES 6 TO 8 SERVINGS**

¼ cup extra-virgin olive oil, plus more as needed

2 garlic cloves, crushed with the side of a knife

1 bunch (8 to 10 ounces) green leaf escarole, trimmed, rinsed, and cut into 1-inch pieces

2 cups diced (¼-inch pieces) peeled butternut or other winter squash

12 ounces dried pasta

1 tablespoon coarse salt

16 ounces (1 large container) whole-milk ricotta

1 cup grated Parmigiano-Reggiano

1 teaspoon ground cinnamon

6 ounces mozzarella cheese, cut into ¼-inch cubes

1 Heat the oil and garlic in a large, deep skillet or wide saucepan until the garlic begins to sizzle. Reduce the heat to low and cook, stirring, until the garlic begins to turn golden but not brown, about 2 minutes. Add the escarole, still wet from rinsing, and stir to blend. Cover and cook, tossing with tongs at least once, until the escarole is wilted and tender, about 10 minutes. Remove from the heat, uncover, and let stand. Do not drain.

2 Place the squash in a steamer basket in a saucepan over boiling water. Steam, covered, until tender, about 10 minutes. Add to the pan with the escarole.

3 Preheat the oven to 350°F. Bring a large pot almost filled with water to a boil. Add

the pasta and salt and cook, stirring occasionally, until the pasta is firm to the bite, 8 to 12 minutes depending on the shape. Ladle out 1 cup of the pasta cooking water and reserve. Drain the pasta and add to the escarole and squash.

4 In a bowl, whisk together the ricotta, the reserved pasta cooking water, ½ cup of the Parmigiano-Reggiano, and the cinnamon until blended. Add the mozzarella and stir to blend. Add to the pasta mixture and fold until well blended.

5 Lightly oil a 13-x-9-inch baking dish. Spread the pasta mixture in the baking dish. Sprinkle with the remaining ½ cup Parmigiano-Reggiano. Bake until the pasta is golden, 25 to 30 minutes. Let stand for 10 minutes before serving.

Noodles with Yogurt and Mint Sauce

These hot noodles in butter and yogurt evoke a dish I used to eat years ago at a favorite Afghani restaurant in New York City. Typically the noodles are tossed with a meaty tomato sauce, but I prefer to serve them nestled in a pool of creamy yogurt and mint sauce. The mint adds just the right hit of freshness. If the yogurt is too tangy for your taste, add a tiny drizzle of honey (less than 1 tablespoon) to tame some of the acidity. MAKES 4 SERVINGS

4 tablespoons (½ stick) unsalted butter

1 teaspoon grated garlic

2 cups plain whole-milk yogurt, stirred until smooth

2 tablespoons minced fresh mint leaves, plus more if desired

Scant tablespoon honey (optional)

8 ounces egg noodles

1 tablespoon coarse salt

2 tablespoons finely chopped pistachios (optional)

1 Melt the butter in a medium skillet. Stir in the garlic and cook over low heat until the garlic sizzles and the butter foams, but do not brown the garlic, about 1 minute. Remove from the heat. Stir in the yogurt, mint, and honey (if using) until blended and set aside, covered.

2 Bring a large pot three quarters filled with water to a boil. Stir in the noodles and salt and cook, stirring to keep the noodles from sticking, until the noodles are tender, 8 to 10 minutes. Drain in a colander and immediately return to the hot pot. Stir in the yogurt sauce until blended.

3 Spoon the noodles into shallow pasta bowls and sprinkle each with some of the pistachios and more mint, if desired.

Summer Squash Pastitsio

A Greek-style mac 'n' cheese, this dish is made with bucatini, a thick, hollow spaghetti, and two sauces—one with sautéed zucchini and onion simmered in tomatoes and the other a creamy sauce made with half-and-half and Roasted Vegetable Broth. Heady with the flavor of cinnamon and allspice, pastitsio is a classic dish in Greece, but according to author Diane Kochilas, an authority on Greek cooking, it has Italian roots. Typically made with lamb, this version is very successful using all vegetables. Look for the delicious hard grating cheese of Greece called Kefalotyri for this dish. If unavailable, you can substitute Parmigiano-Reggiano.

MAKES 6 TO 8 SERVINGS

Zucchini-Tomato Sauce

- 2 tablespoons extra-virgin olive oil
- 1 cup sliced (¼-inch) onion
- 2 garlic cloves, smashed with the side of a knife
- 3 medium zucchini, trimmed and cut into small (2-x-¼-inch) sticks (about 4 cups)
- ½ teaspoon coarse salt
- ¼ teaspoon freshly ground black pepper
- 2 cups Roasted Plum Tomatoes (page 103), pureed in a food processor or blender, or canned crushed tomatoes
- ¾ teaspoon dried oregano
- ½ teaspoon ground cinnamon
- ½ teaspoon ground allspice
- ½ cup coarsely shredded Kefalotyri (see page 265) or Parmigiano-Reggiano

Béchamel Sauce

- ¼ cup extra-virgin olive oil
- ¼ cup all-purpose flour
- 2 cups half-and-half or whole milk
- 1 cup Roasted Vegetable Broth (page 120)
- 2 egg yolks
- ½ teaspoon ground cinnamon
- ½ teaspoon ground allspice
- ½ teaspoon coarse salt
- ¼ teaspoon freshly ground black pepper
- ½ cup coarsely shredded Kefalotyri or Parmigiano-Reggiano

Assembly

- 12 ounces bucatini or other thick spaghetti
- 1 tablespoon coarse salt
- 1 cup coarsely shredded Kefalotyri or Parmigiano-Reggiano

....

1 Make the Zucchini-Tomato Sauce: Heat the oil in a large skillet until hot enough to sizzle a piece of onion. Add the onion and garlic and cook, stirring, over medium-low heat until wilted and golden, about 10 minutes. Add the zucchini, salt, and pepper and cook, stirring, until the zucchini is almost tender, about 10 minutes. Add the tomato puree, oregano, cinnamon, and allspice. Simmer, uncovered, for about 10 minutes. Stir in the cheese. Set aside in the skillet.

2 **Make the Béchamel Sauce:** Warm the oil in a medium saucepan. Stir in the flour and cook, stirring, over medium-low heat, until bubbly. Reduce the heat to low and cook, stirring, for about 3 minutes. Gradually add the half-and-half, whisking constantly until the sauce is smooth and begins to thicken. Whisk in the broth and cook, stirring, for about 5 minutes.

3 Beat the yolks in a small bowl. Whisk about ½ cup of the hot cream sauce into the yolks to temper them. Add the tempered egg yolk mixture to the pan with the cream sauce, whisking until blended. Remove from the heat. Whisk in the cinnamon, allspice, salt, and pepper. Stir in the cheese and set aside.

4 **Assemble the casserole:** Preheat the oven to 350°F. Lightly oil a shallow 2-quart baking dish.

5 Bring a large pot of water to a boil. Add the bucatini and salt and stir to separate the strands. Cook until the bucatini is al dente, or firm to the bite, 8 to 10 minutes. Drain and return to the pot. Transfer half of the cooked bucatini to the skillet with the zucchini sauce and stir to combine. Spread in the bottom of the prepared baking dish.

6 Add the reserved Béchamel Sauce to the remaining bucatini. Stir in ½ cup of the cheese and stir to combine. Spoon on top of the zucchini sauce mixture in the baking dish. Sprinkle with the remaining ½ cup cheese.

7 Bake until the top is browned and the casserole is bubbly, about 35 minutes. Let cool for about 15 minutes before cutting into squares and serving.

Greek Cheeses

Kefalotyri A hard grating or shredding cheese with a nutty taste. It is delicious lightly coated with crumbs and sautéed until golden in olive oil.

Manouri A molded creamy cheese that melts on your tongue like butter.

Kasseri A yellow cow's-milk cheese similar to Comté or Gruyère in texture.

Mizithra Made from the whey left from feta mixed with whole milk. Depending on aging, it is available fresh and soft or very hard and crumbly.

Chickpeas and Pasta
with Artichoke Hearts

Growing up in an Italian Catholic family, we enjoyed a meatless Friday night supper: a comforting dish of chickpeas and elbow macaroni called *ceci e pasta*. A small amount of pasta cooking water is added to the braised vegetables to make the sauce, creating an almost stewlike dish.

MAKES 4 SERVINGS

¼ cup extra-virgin olive oil

1 bag (12 ounces) or box (10 ounces) frozen artichoke hearts, thawed

1 cup thinly sliced onion

1 cup thinly sliced celery, plus 2 tablespoons chopped celery leaves

1 cup thinly sliced peeled carrot

2 garlic cloves, coarsely chopped

1 teaspoon dried oregano

1 teaspoon coarse salt

Freshly ground black pepper

½ cup dried elbow pasta

1 can (15 ounces) chickpeas, drained, or 1½ cups cooked dried chickpeas

1 can (14.5 ounces) diced tomatoes with their juices

1 tablespoon tomato paste

¼ cup chopped (⅛-inch pieces) Parmigiano-Reggiano

1 Combine the oil, artichokes, onion, celery, celery leaves, carrot, garlic, oregano, salt, and a generous grinding of black pepper in a large, deep skillet or sauté pan with a lid. Cook, stirring, over medium heat until the vegetables begin to sizzle. Reduce the heat to low and cook, covered, until the vegetables are wilted but not browned, about 15 minutes.

2 Meanwhile, cook the pasta in a saucepan filled with salted boiling water until tender, about 10 minutes. Ladle out 1½ cups of the pasta cooking water and reserve. Drain the pasta.

3 Stir the cooked pasta, half (¾ cup) of the reserved pasta cooking water, chickpeas, tomatoes, and tomato paste into the vegetables. Add the Parmigiano-Reggiano. Cook, covered, over low heat for about 10 minutes to blend the flavors. Add more of the reserved pasta cooking water if you'd prefer the mixture to be soupier. Serve ladled into bowls.

Toasted Israeli Couscous with Sautéed Mushrooms, Cauliflower, and Peas

I didn't know the story behind Israeli couscous until I read Joan Nathan's *The Foods of Israel Today*. In the 1950s, as an influx of Jews from Middle Eastern countries came to Israel, the foods they were accustomed to eating—primarily rice and couscous—were in short supply. An enterprising noodle manufacturer, who had immigrated to Israel from what is now the Czech Republic, came up with two extruded pasta shapes, one that resembles rice and one that resembles couscous (popularly known as Israeli couscous, although sometimes called pearl couscous). **MAKES 4 TO 6 SERVINGS**

3 tablespoons extra-virgin olive oil

½ cup diced onion

8 ounces cremini, white button, stemmed shiitake, or other mushrooms, diced (about 3 cups)

2 cups 1-inch cauliflower florets

1 teaspoon ground cumin

1½ teaspoons coarse salt

Freshly ground black pepper

1 cup frozen peas, thawed

2 cups Israeli couscous

4 cups water

1 tablespoon fresh lemon juice

1 tablespoon finely chopped fresh mint (optional)

1 Heat 2 tablespoons of the oil in a wok or deep skillet with a lid. Add the onion and cook, stirring, until golden brown, about 5 minutes. Add the mushrooms and cauliflower and cook, stirring frequently, until the mushrooms are golden and the cauliflower is almost tender, 10 to 12 minutes. Stir in the cumin, ½ teaspoon of the salt, and a generous grinding of pepper. Stir in the peas and cook for about 1 minute. Spoon the cooked vegetables into a bowl and cover with foil to keep warm.

2 Add the couscous and the remaining 1 tablespoon oil to the skillet. Cook, stirring, over medium heat, until the couscous is golden brown, about 5 minutes. Add the water and the remaining 1 teaspoon salt and bring to a boil. Stir once, cover, and cook over medium-high heat until all the water is absorbed and the couscous is tender, 18 to 20 minutes.

3 Add the cooked vegetables to the couscous and gently fold together until blended. Sprinkle with the lemon juice and mint, if using. Serve at once.

Goat Cheese–Stuffed
Baked Tomatoes with
Herbes de Provence,
page 306

VEGETABLE SIDES

Spiced Roasted Beets with Toasted Almond Skordalia Sauce

Roasting beets, instead of steaming or boiling them, concentrates their flavor. Here they are roasted with vinegar and spices in a covered casserole. The timing will vary, depending on the age and size of the beets. They can be roasted ahead, peeled, sliced, and served warm, at room temperature, or cold. The skordalia is a sauce made from a puree of day-old bread, olive oil, garlic, lemon, and finely chopped nuts. In addition to serving it with beets, I like it spooned over thick slices of roasted eggplant or halved zucchini, or as a dip for raw vegetables. The pungency of the garlic will mellow as the sauce stands. MAKES 4 SERVINGS

3 or 4 large beets (about 2½ pounds)

8 whole cloves

1 teaspoon whole peppercorns

1 bay leaf

½ cup red wine vinegar

1½ teaspoons coarse salt, plus more as needed

¾ to 1¼ cups water, plus more as needed

½ cup slivered almonds

2 cups cubed (½-inch pieces) day-old Italian bread with crusts removed

1 tablespoon finely chopped garlic

½ cup plus 2 tablespoons extra-virgin olive oil

¼ cup fresh lemon juice

1 tablespoon finely chopped fresh parsley, dill, or mint, or a combination

1 Preheat the oven to 350°F. Place the beets in a deep casserole. Add the cloves, peppercorns, bay leaf, vinegar, ½ teaspoon of the salt, and ½ cup of the water. Cover with a lid or aluminum foil and roast for about 1 hour, checking the level of liquid after about 45 minutes. If dry, add another ½ cup water. Check the doneness of the beets with the tip of a paring knife. If firm, roast for 15 to 30 minutes longer, or until the beets are tender. Set aside at room temperature.

2 While the beets are roasting use the oven to toast the almonds: Spread the almonds in a small baking pan or pie plate and toast in the oven until lightly browned, about 12 minutes. Set aside.

3 When the beets are cool enough to handle, slip off the skins and trim the rough parts. Cut the beets into ½-inch-thick rounds, wedges, or cubes. Place in a shallow serving bowl. Cover with foil and keep warm in an oven set at the lowest temperature, or keep at room temperature, or, if you prefer to serve the beets cold, place in the refrigerator until ready to serve.

4 Place the bread cubes in a bowl and sprinkle with the remaining ¼ cup water. Let stand for about 10 minutes. Rub the wet bread with your hands until it is crumbled. You should have about ½ cup lightly packed.

5 Combine the almonds, garlic, and remaining 1 teaspoon salt in a food processor and process until pulverized. Add the wet bread crumbs and pulse until well blended. Combine the oil and lemon juice and gradually add in a steady stream, pulsing until thoroughly blended and the mixture is smooth. If the sauce is very thick, add water, 1 tablespoon at a time, pulsing after each addition, until the sauce is moderately thick and smooth. Taste and add more salt, if needed.

6 Spoon or spread the sauce over the beets and garnish with the herbs.

Broccolini with Chinese Salted Black Beans

The distinctive tangy taste of Chinese black beans, which are salted and fermented soybeans, stands up well to an assertive-tasting vegetable such as broccolini. Broccolini has long, slender stems that stay crunchy minutes after the clusters of loose florets at the top turn tender. Chinese black beans can be very salty, so they benefit from a thorough rinsing or a short soak in cold water before using. **MAKES 2 OR 3 SERVINGS**

2 teaspoons salted Chinese black beans

1 tablespoon vegetable oil

1 tablespoon finely chopped garlic

1 tablespoon soy sauce

1 tablespoon plus 1 teaspoon unseasoned Japanese rice vinegar

1 tablespoon toasted sesame oil (see page 221)

1 pound broccolini, tips of stems trimmed

Pinch of coarse salt

1 Place the beans in a small bowl and cover with cold water; let stand for about 10 minutes. Drain, rinse, and blot dry with a folded paper towel. Finely chop the beans and set aside.

2 Combine the vegetable oil and garlic in a small skillet and slowly heat the oil, stirring, until the garlic begins to sizzle. Lower the heat and cook the garlic, stirring, until it begins to color and is tender, about 1 minute. Do not brown. Remove the skillet from the heat. Add the beans, soy sauce, vinegar, and sesame oil, stir to blend, and set aside.

3 Bring a large, deep skillet half filled with water to a boil. Add the broccolini and a generous pinch of salt. Cook over high heat, uncovered, until the broccolini reaches the desired tenderness, 6 to 8 minutes. Drain well and wipe the skillet dry. Return the broccolini to the skillet, spoon the black bean sauce over the broccolini, and bring to a boil, turning the broccolini in the sauce to coat, about 1 minute.

4 Place the broccolini on a platter and spoon the sauce evenly on top. Serve warm or at room temperature.

Colcannon with Cauliflower

Colcannon, traditionally potatoes mashed with cabbage, is the iconic dish of Ireland. There are many variations, ranging from kale colcannon to leek. Here I've used cauliflower in place of the cabbage, left the potatoes unpeeled, and added a pinch of ground allspice. I love this served with a dollop of prepared mustard. **MAKES 4 SERVINGS**

1½ pounds small Yukon gold potatoes, unpeeled, cut into ¾-inch cubes

1 bay leaf

1 teaspoon coarse salt

12 ounces (about ½ large head) cauliflower, cut into 1-inch chunks, including part of the core

¼ cup whole milk, half-and-half, or heavy cream

4 tablespoons (½ stick) unsalted butter

⅛ teaspoon ground allspice

Freshly ground black pepper

¼ cup thinly sliced scallion (green parts only)

Prepared mustard, for serving (optional)

1 Combine the potatoes, bay leaf, salt, and plenty of water to cover in a medium saucepan. Bring to a boil, cover, and cook for about 10 minutes. Add the cauliflower and cook until the potatoes and cauliflower are both tender, about 10 minutes more. Ladle out ¼ cup of the vegetable cooking liquid and reserve. Drain the vegetables, remove and discard the bay leaf, and return to the saucepan.

2 Add the milk and butter and mash with a potato masher until the mixture is roughly mashed. If it is too thick, thin with the reserved cooking liquid. Sprinkle with the allspice and add a grinding of pepper. Fold in the scallion tops and serve with dribbles of mustard on top, if desired.

Cauliflower, Green Beans, and Butternut Squash with Tomatoes and Cashews

Typical of the Indian kitchen, frying the whole spices—cumin and brown mustard seeds—in hot oil adds a deep spicy, nutty taste to the tomato sauce. The three vegetables in the stew contribute different textures and flavor profiles: sweet, soft butternut squash; crunchy florets of cauliflower; and firm, fresh green beans. **MAKES 4 SERVINGS**

2 tablespoons extra-virgin olive oil

½ cup unsalted raw cashews

1½ teaspoons cumin seeds

1 teaspoon brown mustard seeds

1 cup chopped onion

4 teaspoons grated peeled fresh ginger

1 can (15 ounces) diced tomatoes with their juices

1 serrano or other small green chile, halved and seeded

1 head (about 1½ pounds) cauliflower, cut into 1-inch florets

1 pound butternut squash, peeled, seeded, and cut into 1-inch chunks

¼ to ½ cup water

8 ounces green beans, trimmed, cut into 1-inch lengths

1 teaspoon coarse salt

½ cup plain low-fat or whole-milk yogurt

1 Heat a skillet over medium heat until hot enough to sizzle a drop of water. Add the oil and heat until shimmering. Add the cashews and fry over medium-low heat, stirring, until lightly browned, about 30 seconds. Transfer to a plate with a slotted spoon.

2 Add the cumin and mustard seeds to the hot oil and heat, stirring, until lightly browned, about 30 seconds. Add the onion and ginger and cook, stirring, until the onion is golden, about 5 minutes.

3 Add the tomatoes and chile and bring to a boil over medium-high heat. Boil until the tomatoes thicken and begin to separate from the oil. Add the cauliflower, squash, and ¼ cup water and stir to combine. Cook, covered, over medium-low heat until the vegetables are almost tender, 10 to 15 minutes. Add another ¼ cup water, if needed. Add the green beans and salt and cook, covered, until tender, about 5 minutes. Top with the cashews and serve with a spoonful of yogurt on each serving.

Dry-Fried Green Beans with Ground Peanuts, Tomatoes, and Curry

With one foot in Africa and another in India, this simple dry-fried green bean dish is delicious served over a bowl of rice or eaten as a side dish with other vegetable favorites. Dry-frying is a simple technique of "frying" in a hot pan with little or no oil. To ensure the tenderness of the beans, I generally boil them first very briefly to soften any of the overmature membranes in the pods. MAKES 4 SERVINGS

¼ cup unsalted dry-roasted peanuts

1 pound green beans, stem ends trimmed

1 tablespoon peanut or other vegetable oil

½ cup fresh chopped ripe tomato or canned diced tomatoes, juices drained

2 teaspoons Madras curry powder (see box)

1 garlic clove, grated

1 dried chile pepper (optional)

1 Place the peanuts in a small skillet and cook over medium heat, stirring, until the peanuts begin to change color. Transfer to a side dish and let cool. Grind the cooled peanuts in a food processor and set aside.

2 Bring a large saucepan of water to a boil. Add the green beans and cook, stirring, until barely tender, about 3 minutes. Drain; spread on a kitchen towel and pat dry. Place the green beans and oil in a large bowl and toss to coat the green beans.

3 In a small bowl, stir together the tomatoes, curry powder, and garlic. Set aside.

4 Meanwhile, heat a large skillet or wok over very high heat until hot enough to sizzle and evaporate a drop of water. Add the green beans, a few at a time (they should sizzle), and the chile, if using. Stir-fry the green beans, watching carefully and making sure they continue to sizzle, until each is blistered with small black bubbles, 5 to 8 minutes.

5 Add the tomato mixture and stir to coat. Spoon into a serving dish and sprinkle with the ground peanuts.

Madras Curry Powder

Curry, or masala, is a blend of spices that varies from region to region of India and from cook to cook. I have a preference for Madras curry powder, a blend I can find in my market in a tall, square, bright yellow tin, which seems to contain many "warming" spices such as cinnamon, clove, dried red pepper, and so on in the proportions that I like.

Green Beans with Miso-Sesame Sauce

For a pretty presentation, leave the gracefully tapered end (it's called the blossom end) of the green beans intact. For this dish, I prefer white miso because its slightly sweet taste helps balance the acidity of the vinegar. Look for tall jars of tan sesame seeds in Asian markets. Do not use the pale white sesame seeds for this dish. **MAKES 4 SERVINGS**

2 tablespoons plus 1 teaspoon tan sesame seeds (see page 60)

¼ cup unseasoned Japanese rice vinegar

2 tablespoons white miso paste

1 pound long, slender green beans, stem ends trimmed

1 teaspoon coarse salt

1 Grind 2 tablespoons of the sesame seeds in a spice grinder or with a mortar and pestle until they reach a powdery consistency.

2 Combine the ground sesame seeds, vinegar, and miso in a small bowl and whisk until well blended. Set aside.

3 Bring a large saucepan three quarters filled with water to a boil. Add the green beans and salt and boil until the green beans are tender to the bite, 6 to 8 minutes. Drain well.

4 Place the green beans in a shallow serving bowl and spoon the sauce on top. Garnish with the remaining 1 teaspoon sesame seeds.

Eggplant with Saffron Tomatoes

Instead of frying the eggplant in oil, I slather the slices with oil and brown them in a hot oven. Serve on bulgur rice pilaf. My favorite is Basmati Rice with Caramelized Yellow Onions on page 233. **MAKES 4 SERVINGS**

1 eggplant (1 to 1½ pounds), trimmed, peeled, and cut into ¾-inch-thick slices

Extra-virgin olive oil

¼ cup boiling water

½ teaspoon saffron threads

2 cups thinly sliced onion

2 garlic cloves, bruised with the side of a knife

¾ teaspoon ground turmeric

1 can (28 ounces) diced tomatoes with juices

1 cinnamon stick

¼ cup coarsely chopped fresh flat-leaf (Italian) parsley

2 tablespoons chopped fresh dill

2 tablespoons chopped fresh mint leaves or 2 teaspoons dried mint leaves

1 teaspoon coarse salt, or to taste

1 tablespoon harissa, store-bought or homemade (see page 72), or to taste

1 tablespoon honey

1 tablespoon finely chopped Moroccan Preserved Lemons (page 305)

1 Preheat the oven to 400°F. Arrange the eggplant slices on a large baking sheet. With a brush, coat the eggplant liberally with oil. You will need about ¼ cup. Roast the eggplant until browned on the bottom, about 20 minutes. With a wide spatula, turn the slices over and roast for about 10 minutes more. Remove from the oven.

2 Meanwhile, in a small bowl, combine the boiling water and saffron and let stand for 10 minutes.

3 While the eggplant is roasting, heat 2 tablespoons oil in a deep skillet or wide saucepan. Add the onion and garlic and cook, stirring, over medium-low heat until the onions are a pale golden color, about 10 minutes. Stir in the turmeric and cook for about 1 minute. Add the tomatoes, saffron and water mixture, and cinnamon stick. Bring to a boil, reduce the heat, and simmer for about 20 minutes, or until thickened.

4 Finely chop the parsley, dill, and mint together and add to the sauce. Stir in the salt, harissa, and honey, adjusting the amount of harissa to your taste. Transfer the eggplant slices to the sauce and spoon the sauce over the slices. Cover and cook on low for about 30 minutes. Do not boil.

5 Taste and adjust the seasoning, adding more honey, salt as needed, and/or harissa for a spicier taste. Sprinkle with the Moroccan Preserved Lemon.

Fried Eggplant and Roasted Long Peppers in Tomato and Pomegranate Sauce

Long, narrow Japanese eggplants or smaller Italian globe eggplants are perfect for this dish, in which pomegranate molasses lends a pungent sweet-sour flavor to the sauce. Serve as a side dish with a bulgur pilaf or as a topping over baked potatoes, cooked rice, polenta, pasta, or plain cooked bulgur or couscous. MAKES 4 SERVINGS

4 small Japanese eggplants or 2 small globe eggplants (about 1½ pounds), trimmed, peeled, and cut lengthwise into ½-inch wedges

1 tablespoon coarse salt, plus more to taste

4 long Italian frying peppers or other long green (or multicolored) peppers

2 pounds tomatoes or 1 large can (28 ounces) canned diced plum tomatoes with their juices

Extra-virgin olive oil

2 cups thinly sliced onion

1 garlic clove, grated or pounded into a paste with some coarse salt

½ teaspoon ground cumin

1 dried red chile pepper (optional)

2 tablespoons pomegranate molasses (see page 26)

2 tablespoons coarsely chopped fresh flat-leaf (Italian) parsley

2 tablespoons coarsely chopped fresh mint leaves

1 In a large bowl, toss the eggplant with the salt. Transfer to a colander set over a large bowl. Top the eggplant with a small plate and weight it down with a large can of tomatoes or other heavy item. Let stand for about 1 hour. Rinse the eggplant with cold water to remove excess salt. Wrap in a kitchen towel and press to blot out as much water as possible.

2 Meanwhile, preheat the broiler, positioning the rack so that the tops of the peppers will be about 3 inches from the heat source. Line a baking sheet with a large piece of foil. Arrange the peppers on the foil and broil, turning every 5 minutes, until the peppers are evenly blistered. Wrap the peppers in the foil and let stand until cool enough to handle. Rub off the skins. Halve the peppers, discard the stems and seeds, and cut the flesh into ½-inch-wide strips. Set aside.

3 If using fresh tomatoes, bring a medium saucepan half filled with water to a boil. Score the blossom end of the tomato with a small X. Place the tomatoes in the boiling water and simmer until the skins begin to peel back, 2 to 3 minutes. Transfer to a large plate with a slotted spoon and let cool slightly. Peel off and discard the skins. Place a strainer over a bowl. Crush the tomatoes, one at a time, in your hand over the strainer, squeezing out the seeds and juices into the strainer. Set the flesh aside. Press the seeds against the strainer with the back of a large spoon to extract as much of the juice as possible. Discard the seeds. Chop the flesh and stir into the tomato juices. You should have about 3 cups. If using canned tomatoes, skip this step.

4 Heat a large skillet over medium-high heat until hot enough to evaporate a drop of water. Add enough oil to generously coat the bottom of the pan and heat until shimmering and hot enough to sizzle a piece of eggplant. Add the eggplant. Cook, adjusting the heat to maintain a steady sizzle and turning the pieces, until the eggplant is evenly browned on all sides. As the eggplant browns, remove to a side dish.

5 Add the onions to the skillet, adding a little more oil if necessary. Cook the onions, stirring, over medium heat until golden, about 10 minutes. Stir in the garlic and cumin and cook for about 30 seconds. Add the tomato and juice and bring to a boil. Stir in the eggplant and the roasted pepper. Add the dried chile, if using. Simmer over medium heat until the sauce thickens and the eggplant is very tender, about 20 minutes. Stir in the pomegranate molasses. Taste and add salt, if needed. Finely chop the parsley and mint together and then stir the herbs into the eggplant mixture. Serve hot, at room temperature, or chilled.

Glazed Eggplant

Easy and elegant, this pan-seared Japanese eggplant is glazed with a bit of shoyu (Japanese for soy sauce), miso, and mirin. Mirin is a sweet wine made from glutinous rice available in most supermarkets. Japanese use mirin in cooking to add sweetness, which, in this recipe, balances the salty miso and shoyu. I often use tamari in place of soy sauce; it is similar but thicker, rich, and very dark. Serve the eggplant with its juices over hot steamed white or brown rice. **MAKES 4 SERVINGS**

3 long, thin Japanese eggplants (about 1½ pounds)

¼ cup toasted sesame oil (see page 221)

3 tablespoons red miso paste

3 tablespoons water

3 tablespoons soy sauce or tamari (see page 44)

3 tablespoons mirin (sweet rice wine)

2 to 4 thin slices jalapeño or other green chile pepper

½ teaspoon tan sesame seeds (see page 60)

1 Trim the eggplants and quarter them. Cut each piece in half crosswise.

2 Heat the oil in a large, heavy skillet over high heat until rippling. Add the eggplant, cut sides down, and cook, turning and adjusting the heat to keep the eggplant from burning, until well browned, about 6 minutes. With tongs, turn each piece of eggplant skin side down and cook until blistered, about 5 minutes more.

3 Meanwhile, in a small bowl, whisk together the miso and water until smooth. Add the soy sauce and mirin. Add to the skillet, turning the eggplant until evenly coated, and cook until the liquid has thickened and mostly evaporated, about 2 minutes.

4 Transfer the eggplant to a shallow bowl. Add the jalapeño to the juices remaining in the skillet and stir to blend. Drizzle the juices over the eggplant. Sprinkle with the sesame seeds. Serve hot or at room temperature.

Winter Greens with Garlic-Toasted Walnuts and Lemon

I first tasted this seductive dish in an Armenian restaurant in St. Petersburg, Russia. The greens are cooked in olive oil, and topped with walnut halves that have been warmed in olive oil and then tossed with grated garlic and salt. MAKES 4 SERVINGS

1 large garlic clove, grated

½ teaspoon coarse salt

4 tablespoons extra-virgin olive oil

½ cup walnut halves

6 ounces kale

6 ounces Swiss chard

6 ounces escarole

6 ounces large spinach leaves

1 teaspoon grated lemon zest

1 tablespoon fresh lemon juice

2 tablespoons chopped fresh dill (optional)

1 Mash the garlic and salt together with the back of a spoon and set aside. Heat 2 tablespoons of the oil in a large skillet with a lid. Add the walnuts and sauté, stirring, over medium to medium-low heat until the walnuts are golden brown. Remove from the heat. If the oil is very hot, allow it to cool slightly so the garlic doesn't brown when added. Add the garlic and salt and stir to coat. With a spoon, remove the walnuts to a side dish.

2 Pull the ruffled parts of the leaves from the stems of the kale and Swiss chard. Discard the tougher stems (or slice them and save to add to soup). Stack the more tender stems and cut them into ¼-inch slices. Set aside. Cut the leaves crosswise into 1-inch pieces. Cut the core from the escarole and trim the long stems from the spinach if they are tough. Tear the spinach and escarole into 1-inch pieces. You should have a total of 8 to 10 cups packed greens. Rinse well in cold water and drain.

3 Add the remaining 2 tablespoons oil to the skillet and heat until hot enough to sizzle a piece of chard or other green. Add all of the damp greens and the sliced chard stems to the oil, toss with tongs, and cook over medium heat until they begin to sizzle and wilt. Cover and cook over medium-low heat until tender and wilted, 5 to 8 minutes. Uncover and cook until the excess moisture is evaporated. Stir in the lemon zest and juice.

4 Using tongs or a large fork, transfer the cooked greens to a serving dish and top with the dill, if using, and the garlic walnuts.

Okra and Sweet Potatoes in Curried Tomato Sauce

This recipe reflects the rich culinary heritage—specifically African and Indian—of the Caribbean islands. Sweet potatoes and okra are the main ingredients, pulled together in a rich tomato-based sauce laced with a blend of spices found in many powdered curry mixtures. If possible, use fresh okra, although if you're careful not to overcook it, frozen okra is a convenient substitution. Inhabitants of the Caribbean islands like their food fiery with chiles, especially habanero. I find habanero to be too hot, so I am happier with the subtle heat of a minced jalapeño. But if you like hot, go for it. **MAKES 4 SERVINGS**

1 pound small fresh okra, tips of stems trimmed, left whole, or 1 package (10 ounces) frozen whole or sliced okra

2 tablespoons vegetable oil or ghee (see page 76)

½ cup chopped onion

½ cup chopped green bell pepper

1 tablespoon finely chopped peeled fresh ginger

1 to 2 teaspoons minced jalapeño or habanero or other hotter chile pepper, if desired

1 teaspoon ground cumin

½ teaspoon ground coriander

½ teaspoon ground cinnamon

½ teaspoon turmeric

⅛ teaspoon ground allspice

1 can (14.5 ounces) diced tomatoes with their juices

½ cup water

2 cups diced peeled sweet potato

2 tablespoons raisins

2 tablespoons finely chopped fresh cilantro

1 Add the okra to a steamer basket, set over boiling water, cover, and steam until crisp-tender, 3 to 4 minutes. Remove the steamer from the saucepan and let the okra stand until ready to use. Do not rinse with water.

2 Heat the oil in a medium skillet over medium heat until hot enough to sizzle a piece of onion. Add the onion and bell pepper and cook, stirring, until the onion is golden and the peppers are tender, about 5 minutes. Add the ginger, chile, cumin, coriander, cinnamon, turmeric, and allspice and heat, stirring, for about 30 seconds. Add the tomatoes. Rinse the tomato can

with the ½ cup water, add it to the vegetable mixture, and simmer over low heat, uncovered, for about 5 minutes.

3 Stir in the sweet potatoes and raisins and cook over medium-low heat, covered, until the sweet potatoes are tender when pierced with the tip of a knife, about 10 minutes. Add 1 tablespoon of the cilantro. Add the okra and fold gently only once or twice to avoid releasing the okra juice, which would make the texture of the okra slippery. Sprinkle with the remaining 1 tablespoon cilantro before serving.

Garlic and Parsley Oven-Fried Potatoes

These irresistible sizzling sticks of crisp oven-fried potatoes are tossed with a finely chopped mixture of raw garlic and parsley and a shower of salt. They are a staple throughout Argentina, especially at outdoor barbecue restaurants, and so beloved they even show up in sandwiches, tucked between thick rolls or slices of bread. For the best flavor, be sure to use very finely chopped fresh (not old sprouted or jarred) garlic. **MAKES 4 SERVINGS**

1½ pounds long white all-purpose potatoes (not russets), peeled

¼ cup extra-virgin olive oil

3 tablespoons very finely chopped fresh flat-leaf (Italian) parsley

1 to 2 teaspoons very finely chopped garlic

1 to 2 teaspoons high-quality finishing sea salt or coarse salt, to taste

1 Place a large baking sheet on the bottom rack of the oven and set the temperature to 450°F. Preheat the oven and the pan for 15 minutes.

2 Meanwhile, cut the potatoes first lengthwise into ¼-inch-thick slices and then into ¼-inch-wide sticks. Rinse off the starch from the surface of the potatoes, drain, spread them on a kitchen towel, and pat dry. Place in a bowl and toss with the oil.

3 Once the baking sheet is very hot, carefully remove it from the oven and spread the potatoes evenly on the pan. The potatoes should sizzle. Immediately return the pan to the oven and oven-fry the potatoes until browned on the bottom, about 20 minutes. Remove the pan from the oven and with a wide spatula turn the potatoes, moving the potatoes from the outer edges to the middle of the pan and the potatoes in the middle of the pan to the edges. Oven-fry until the potatoes are nicely browned, 10 to 12 minutes more.

4 Meanwhile, mix the parsley and garlic together in a small bowl. When the potatoes are nicely browned, remove them from the oven and transfer to a large bowl. Add the parsley mixture and a generous shower of the salt. Toss to coat. The hot potatoes will partially cook the garlic. Serve at once.

Mexican Roasted Potato Spears with Melted Cheese

These roasted potatoes are topped with a Mexican semisoft melting cheese similar to mozzarella, which can be substituted. **MAKES 4 SERVINGS**

Achiote Sauce

- 1 garlic clove, chopped
- 1 tablespoon chopped onion
- ½ teaspoon coarse salt
- ½ teaspoon chile powder
- ½ teaspoon grated orange zest
- 1 piece (½-x-¼-inch) adobo de achiote or paste (see box)
- 2 tablespoons fresh orange juice
- 1 tablespoon extra-virgin olive oil

Potatoes

- 2 pounds russet potatoes, scrubbed, unpeeled, cut into long ½-inch-thick spears
- 1 large onion, cut into ½-inch wedges
- 2 cups shredded or slivered Chihuahua or asadero cheese (see page 249), or mozzarella cheese
- 1 avocado, peeled, pitted, and cut into thin wedges (optional)
- 2 tablespoons finely chopped fresh cilantro

1 Preheat the oven to 400°F.

2 **Make the Achiote Sauce:** Place the garlic, onion, salt, chile powder, orange zest, and achiote in a mortar and pound with a pestle until mashed together. Or, finely chop in a mini-chopper or blender until the mixture turns into a paste. Gradually work in the orange juice and oil until blended; set the sauce aside.

3 **Make the potatoes:** In a large bowl, combine the potatoes, onions, and sauce and toss to coat. Spread in a 13-x-9-inch baking dish and roast, turning the potatoes once, until golden and tender, about 45 minutes.

4 Sprinkle the cheese on top of the potatoes and roast until the cheese is melted, about 5 minutes. Spoon the sauce on top. Garnish with the avocado, if using. Sprinkle with the cilantro before serving.

Adobo de Achiote

Achiote is the name for both the deep red seeds of the annatto tree and the spice made from them. The spice adds an earthy taste and a reddish color to dishes. Typically used in the cooking of the Yucatán, achiote is ground into a paste called adobo de achiote. It is packaged in a cellophane block in a small flat box wherever Mexican ingredients are sold.

Whipped Potatoes with Cheese

Called *pommes aligot* in France, this dish of potatoes whipped with cheese is decidedly indulgent. To make a meal that isn't overly rich, eat it accompanied by a green vegetable or salad. I first ate *pommes aligot* at Ambassade d'Auvergne, a restaurant in Paris where the cooks whip up individual copper pans of *aligot* for each order. The whipping continues as the waiter carries the pan to your table. It's a deliciously noisy experience. Traditionally the fresh curds of Cantal, a semi-hard cow's-milk cheese from south central France, are used. Fortunately, any semi-hard melting cheese—Cantal, Comté, Gruyère, Fontina, Raclette, even cheddar or mozzarella—will work. Serve as you would mashed potatoes, or with Crostini (page 23) or pieces of toasted baguette to scoop it up. MAKES 2 TO 4 SERVINGS

2 pounds russet (Idaho) potatoes, peeled and cut into large chunks

1 teaspoon coarse salt

1 cup whole milk, heated

2 tablespoons unsalted butter, softened

1 garlic clove, grated

12 ounces Cantal, Raclette, Gruyère, Comté, or other semi-hard, nutty cow's-milk cheese, coarsely grated or cut into small (¼-inch) pieces

1 Bring the potatoes, salt, and enough water to cover to a boil. Cook the potatoes, partially covered, until tender, 10 to 15 minutes. Drain and return to the pot. Over low heat, mash the potatoes, ½ cup of the milk, the butter, and the garlic with a potato masher until blended. Mash in the remaining ½ cup milk. (Do not puree in a food processor.)

2 Add half of the cheese and beat with a wooden spoon until incorporated. Add the remaining half of the cheese and beat until the potatoes and cheese become stringy. Serve at once, while still hot, directly from the pot, as they do in France.

Roasted Potatoes and Apples with Raclette Cheese

Raclette is a traditional Alpine dish of warm melted cheese served on boiled potatoes. This recipe plays off that idea with roasted potatoes and apples topped with the cheese and broiled until browned and bubbly. Serve with a green salad or a platter of cooked greens and you've got a satisfying meal. MAKES 4 SERVINGS

1 pound all-purpose white potatoes (not russets), peeled and cut into ½-inch wedges

1 pound firm baking apples, such as Granny Smith, Rome Beauties, or other, cut into ½-inch wedges (not peeled)

1 cup thinly sliced onion

3 tablespoons extra-virgin olive oil

½ teaspoon coarse salt

¼ teaspoon freshly grated nutmeg

Freshly ground black pepper

6 ounces Raclette, Italian Fontina, or aged Gruyère, cut into eight ⅛-inch-thick slices

1 Preheat the oven to 400°F.

2 Combine the potatoes, apples, onion, oil, salt, nutmeg, and a grinding of pepper in a 13-x-9-inch broiler-proof baking dish. Toss to combine the ingredients and spread in a single layer.

3 Roast until the potatoes and apples are very tender, 45 to 55 minutes. Remove from the oven and turn the broiler to high.

4 Arrange the cheese slices on top of the roasted potato mixture. Broil until bubbly, 3 to 5 minutes. Serve hot.

Sag Paneer

A popular dish on most Indian restaurant menus, sag paneer is made with a firm white Indian cheese called paneer; *sag* means spinach. Paneer is sold in vacuum-sealed 8-ounce blocks and can be found in the cheese section of most grocery stores. Choose the large sturdy-leaf spinach sold in bunches rather than the delicate baby spinach in bags. The tomato is optional but adds a nice fresh taste, as does the minced hot chile. MAKES 4 SERVINGS

1 pound loose-leaf spinach, tough stems trimmed, washed, drained, and coarsely chopped

5 tablespoons ghee (see page 76) or clarified butter or coconut oil

8 ounces paneer, cut into ½-inch squares

1 cup finely chopped onion

2 teaspoons Madras curry powder (see page 279)

½ teaspoon turmeric

½ teaspoon coarse salt

1 to 2 teaspoons finely chopped fresh green or red chile, to taste

1 garlic clove, grated

1 teaspoon grated peeled fresh ginger

1 cup coconut milk

½ cup well-drained chopped fresh or canned tomato (optional)

1 Place the spinach in a steamer basket, set over boiling water, cover, and steam until the spinach is wilted and tender, about 5 minutes. Transfer the spinach in the steamer to a large strainer and press on it with the back of a spoon to remove as much water as possible. (Save the water for soup.) Let the spinach stand until ready to use.

2 Meanwhile, heat 3 tablespoons of the ghee in a large skillet until hot enough to sizzle a piece of the paneer. Add the paneer in a single layer and fry, turning with tongs, until lightly browned on all sides, 2 to 3 minutes per side. Transfer to a side dish.

3 Add the remaining 2 tablespoons ghee until hot enough to sizzle a piece of onion. Add the onion and cook, stirring, over medium heat until golden, about 10 minutes. Stir in the curry powder, turmeric, and salt and cook for about 1 minute. Add the chile, garlic, and ginger.

4 Add the reserved spinach, coconut milk, and tomato, if using, and heat to a gentle simmer. Reduce the heat and cook, uncovered, stirring occasionally, for about 5 minutes. Fold in the fried cheese and serve.

Curried Spinach in Coconut Milk with Tomatoes and Fried Onions

A recipe for curried spinach in an outstanding cookbook, *A Taste of Africa* by Dorinda Hafner, inspired this recipe. Hafner explains that African "spinach" is a leaf of a local root vegetable that differs dramatically from what we call spinach in the United States. I reinterpreted the recipe using large-leaf bunch spinach. If you can find it, New Zealand spinach, a variety with a thick, bumpy surface, available at some farmers' markets, is perfect.

MAKES 4 SERVINGS

Vegetable oil, as needed

2 cups thinly sliced onion

1 tablespoon Madras curry powder (see page 279)

1 can (13.5 ounces) coconut milk

1 pound large-leaf spinach (not baby spinach), stems trimmed, rinsed, and well drained

½ cup fresh or canned seeded and diced tomatoes, well drained

1 Add about ½ inch of oil to a deep 10-inch skillet and heat over medium heat until hot enough to sizzle a piece of onion. Gradually stir in the onions, adjusting the heat as the onions sizzle. Cook until well browned, but not black, 15 to 20 minutes. Lift the onions from the oil with a slotted spoon and set in a strainer set over a bowl.

Do not use paper towels for draining the onions as the paper will make them soggy. Let stand until ready to serve. (If desired, reserve the onion-infused oil for future onion frying or to season other dishes.)

2 In a large, wide saucepan or deep skillet over medium heat, warm the curry powder, stirring, until it becomes fragrant, about 1 minute. Stir in the coconut milk and bring to a boil. Add the spinach all at once. Toss to coat. Cook, covered, until wilted, 3 to 5 minutes.

3 Spoon into a serving dish. Serve at once, garnished with the diced tomatoes and fried onions.

Winter Squash, Corn, and Zucchini Stew with Melted Cheese

This thick vegetable stew is typically made with a dry-fleshed squash called calabaza, also known as West Indian pumpkin. If you live near an ethnic market, you might find it, cut into large 1-pound pieces and wrapped in plastic. The best alternatives are the relatively dry, creamy-fleshed kabocha, hubbard, or butternut squash. The sauce is flavored with sweet paprika, or you might want to use the now-popular smoked paprika (I am partial to pimentón de la Vera) for a slight flavor variation. Serve this stew as a main dish or as a side with cornbread, rice, or polenta.

MAKES 4 TO 6 SERVINGS

2 tablespoons extra-virgin olive oil

2 cups thinly sliced onion

2 teaspoons sweet paprika

1 pound peeled and seeded winter squash, cut into ½-inch cubes (about 2 cups)

1 can (14.5 ounces) diced tomatoes with their juices

1 teaspoon minced jalapeño pepper, or more to taste

1 teaspoon dried oregano

½ teaspoon coarse salt

1 cup fresh or frozen corn kernels

1 cup diced (¼-inch pieces) zucchini

1 cup crumbled or shredded queso blanco or queso fresco cheese (see page 249), or mozzarella

1 Heat the oil in a large skillet over medium-high heat until hot enough to sizzle a piece of onion. Add the onion and cook, stirring, until translucent, about 5 minutes. Add the paprika and cook, stirring, until the onion begins to brown, about 5 minutes more.

2 Add the squash, tomatoes, jalapeño, oregano, and salt and bring to a boil, stirring to combine. Cook, covered, until the squash is tender, about 15 minutes. Uncover and stir occasionally. Add small amounts of water, ¼ cup at a time, if the mixture gets too dry.

3 Stir in the corn and zucchini. Cook, covered, until the vegetables are tender, about 5 minutes. Sprinkle the cheese on top, cover, and cook until the cheese is melted, about 3 minutes.

Sweet Potatoes and Green Beans with Toasted Coconut and Cilantro

Coconut oil can be heated to very hot without smoking or burning and therefore has the ability to create a richly browned surface on these sweet potatoes. A handful of green beans makes a bright visual contrast and a welcome textural experience. Don't hesitate to add a hint of heat in the form of a whole dried chile or a light dusting of cayenne. The sweetness of the potatoes and the caramelized onion both welcome the juxtaposition of something spicy. **MAKES 4 SERVINGS**

2 tablespoons grated unsweetened coconut

½ teaspoon coarse salt

1 cup (about 3 ounces) green beans, stems trimmed, cut into 1-inch lengths

¼ cup coconut oil or vegetable oil

1 teaspoon whole toasted cumin seeds

1 small whole dried red chile

1½ pounds sweet potatoes, peeled and cut into 1-inch chunks (about 6 cups)

1 large onion, cut into ½-inch chunks (about 2 cups)

¾ teaspoon ground turmeric

¼ cup coconut milk, or more to taste

1 teaspoon very finely chopped fresh cilantro (optional)

1 Sprinkle the coconut in a small skillet and heat, stirring, over medium-low heat until it is lightly toasted, about 1 minute. Set aside.

2 Half fill a small saucepan with water and bring to a boil. Add the salt and green beans and cook until the green beans are crisp-tender, 3 to 5 minutes. Drain well and set aside.

3 Combine the coconut oil, cumin, and chile in a large skillet or wok. Heat, stirring, over medium-high heat, until the cumin seeds begin to darken, about 30 seconds.

4 Add the sweet potatoes and onion and cook over medium to medium-high heat, lifting the sweet potatoes as they brown on one side and turning, until the sweet potatoes are well browned and fork-tender, 15 to 20 minutes. Reduce the heat to low, sprinkle with the turmeric, and continue cooking, turning the potatoes, for about 1 minute.

5 Add the green beans and coconut milk and gently turn the potatoes until evenly moistened. Remove the chile, if desired. Sprinkle with the toasted coconut and cilantro, if using, and serve.

Butternut Squash with Toasted Cumin, Chickpeas, and Tomatoes

Variations on this stewlike concoction with Indian flavors are many. Although typically made with potatoes, this version uses butternut squash. Serve a small portion as a side dish with Coconut Milk Rice Pilaf with Cilantro Sauce (page 243). **MAKES 4 SERVINGS**

1 tablespoon diced peeled fresh ginger

2 garlic cloves, coarsely chopped

1 teaspoon coarse salt

3 tablespoons ghee (see page 76), clarified butter, or vegetable or coconut oil

1 teaspoon cumin seeds

1 cup chopped onion

1 can (15 ounces) chickpeas, rinsed and drained

1 can (15 ounces) diced tomatoes with their juices

½ cup water

1 small dried red chile pepper

1 medium butternut squash (about 1¾ pounds), halved lengthwise, seeded, peeled, and cut into ½-inch pieces

¼ cup coarsely chopped fresh cilantro

1 With a mortar and pestle, mash the ginger, garlic, and salt into a paste. If you don't have a mortar and pestle, grate the ginger and garlic into a small bowl. Add the salt and blend with the back of a spoon. Set aside.

2 Heat the ghee in a wide, large saucepan or a deep skillet until very hot. Add the cumin and stir until it begins to change color, about 20 seconds. Reduce the heat to low and add the onion. Cook, stirring, until the onion begins to turn golden, about 10 minutes. Stir in the garlic mixture until blended. Add the chickpeas and cook, stirring, until coated with the seasonings, about 5 minutes.

3 Add the tomatoes, water, and chile. Bring to a boil. Stir in the cubed squash. Cover and cook until the squash is fork-tender, 15 to 20 minutes. Remove the chile, if desired. Sprinkle with the cilantro and serve.

Swiss Chard with Caramelized Red Onion and Moroccan Preserved Lemon

If you don't have preserved lemons on hand, you can approximate the taste by adding a teaspoon of grated lemon zest mashed with $1/2$ teaspoon coarse salt plus $1/2$ tablespoon fresh lemon juice. But I urge you to make Moroccan Preserved Lemons. MAKES 2 OR 3 SERVINGS

1 bunch (about 1 pound) Swiss chard

2 tablespoons extra-virgin olive oil

1 cup thinly sliced red onion

1 tablespoon finely diced rind from Moroccan Preserved Lemons (recipe follows)

1 Rinse the chard and, while still wet, pull the leafy greens from the stems. Reserve the stems for another use. Tear or coarsely cut up the greens. You should have about 8 cups loosely packed.

2 In a 10-inch skillet, heat the oil over medium heat until hot enough to gently sizzle a slice of onion. Add the onion and cook, stirring, until the onion begins to brown and caramelize, about 10 minutes. Add the wet greens to the onions all at once and toss with tongs to blend. Cook, covered, until the greens are tender, about 5 minutes, stirring with tongs once or twice.

3 Sprinkle with the preserved lemon and toss to blend. Serve hot.

Moroccan Preserved Lemons

MAKES ½ PINT

2 or 3 small lemons, preferably organic, scrubbed clean

2 tablespoons coarse salt

⅓ cup fresh lemon juice

1 Trim the ends from the lemons and partially cut into 8 wedges, leaving the wedges attached at one end. Rub the cut surfaces with the salt. Press the lemons back into their original shape. Push into a clean half-pint canning jar. Add enough of the lemon juice to cover the lemons. Wipe off the rim of the jar. Top with the lid and fasten the screw band. Store the jar in a dark place for 3 to 4 weeks, turning it upside down every few days so the salt is distributed evenly.

2 Store in the refrigerator. They will keep for at least 6 months. To use the lemons, separate the pulp from the rind. Finely chop the rind and sprinkle on vegetables, salad, soup, or stew. Finely chop the pulp and add to salad dressing, mayonnaise, or other sauce.

Goat Cheese–Stuffed Baked Tomatoes with Herbes de Provence

Herbes de Provence is a mixture of dried herbs popular in the South of France, typically containing basil, rosemary, sage, lavender, and fennel. It is found in the spice sections in most supermarkets. The other ingredients in this recipe also reflect the cuisine of Provence: fresh goat cheese, fragrant herbs, and vine-ripened tomatoes—the recipe is perfect for the height of tomato season. I prefer less juicy, meatier plum tomatoes, but any tomato can be used. **MAKES 4 SERVINGS**

4 large, ripe plum tomatoes, halved lengthwise

Coarse salt and freshly ground black pepper

Extra-virgin olive oil

5 ounces crumbled goat cheese (about 1 cup)

2 tablespoons finely chopped sweet onion

2 tablespoons coarse dry bread crumbs, preferably homemade

1 small garlic clove, grated

¼ cup coarsely chopped fresh flat-leaf (Italian) parsley

1 teaspoon dried herbes de Provence

1 Preheat the oven to 350°F. Lightly oil a shallow baking dish just large enough to hold the halved tomatoes.

2 With a teaspoon, scoop the seeds and pulp out of the tomatoes. Discard the seeds and chop the remaining pulp. You should have about ½ cup. Place the scooped-out tomatoes in the baking dish. Sprinkle the inside of the tomatoes with salt and a grinding of black pepper.

3 In a medium bowl, combine the tomato pulp, 2 tablespoons oil, the goat cheese, onion, bread crumbs, and garlic.

4 Finely chop the parsley and herbes de Provence together and add to the cheese mixture. Gently toss together with a fork until blended.

5 Spoon the cheese mixture into the tomatoes, dividing evenly and mounding if necessary. Roast until the tomatoes are shriveled and the cheese begins to turn golden, about 35 minutes. Serve warm.

SOURCES

GRAINS AND BEANS
www.amazon.com
www.ansonmills.com 803-476-4122
www.bobsredmill.com 800-349-2173

SPICES
www.wholespice.com 707-778-1750
www.thespicehouse.com 847-328-3711

MIDDLE EASTERN
www.kalustyans.com 800-352-3451
www.efooddepot.com 888-553-5650

ITALIAN
www.markethallfoods.com
888-952-4005
www.gustiamo.com 718-860-2949

MEXICAN AND SPANISH
www.mexgrocer.com 877-463-9476
www.latienda.com 800-710-4304

ASIAN
www.asianfoodgrocer.com
888-482-2742
www.katagiri.com 212-755-3566
(Japanese)

INDIAN
www.ishopindian.com 877-786-8876

CHEESE
www.murrayscheese.com
888-692-4339
www.igourmet.com 877-446-8763

INDEX

Page numbers in *italics* indicate illustrations